UNLEASHING YOUR INNER STRENGTH

The Power of Assertiveness for Women

Daisy Graham

TABLE OF CONTENTS

Introduction

Chapter 1: Understanding Assertiveness

Chapter 3: Effective Communication Skills

- ☐ The role of communication in assertiveness.
- ☐ Understanding the importance of verbal and non-verbal cues.
- ☐ Developing active listening skills.

3.1 Clear and Direct Expression:

- ☐ Communicating thoughts, needs, and boundaries effectively.
- ☐ Using "I" statements to express opinions and preferences.
- ☐ Constructive confrontation and conflict resolution techniques.

3.2 Active Listening and Empathy:

- ☐ Developing attentive listening skills.
- ☐ Demonstrating empathy without compromising assertiveness.
- ☐ Encouraging open and honest communication in others.

Chapter 4: Assertiveness in Various Settings

- ☐ Applying assertiveness skills in different aspects of life.

- [ ] Recognizing the unique challenges women may face in different settings.
- [ ] Strategies for adapting assertiveness to specific situations.

4.1 Assertiveness at Work:
- [ ] Navigating power dynamics and gender bias.
- [ ] Negotiating salary, promotions, and opportunities.
- [ ] Handling difficult conversations and managing conflicts.

4.2 Assertiveness in Relationships:
- [ ] Setting boundaries and expressing needs in personal relationships.
- [ ] Managing assertiveness in intimate partnerships.
- [ ] Handling conflicts and disagreements constructively.

Chapter 5: Overcoming Barriers and Obstacles
- [ ] Identifying common obstacles to assertiveness for women.
- [ ] Strategies for overcoming fear, guilt, and social conditioning.
- [ ] Building resilience in the face of setbacks.

5.1 Assertiveness and Self-Care:
- ☐ Recognizing the importance of self-care in assertiveness.
- ☐ Managing stress and burnout.
- ☐ Prioritizing personal well-being without guilt.

5.2 Seeking Support and Building a Network:
- ☐ Developing a support system of like-minded individuals.
- ☐ Encouraging and empowering other women to be assertive.
- ☐ Collaborating with mentors and role models.

Introduction

Assertiveness plays a crucial role in empowering women to navigate both professional and personal domains with confidence and effectiveness.

Assertiveness is often misunderstood as aggression or passivity, but it is, in fact, a distinct and valuable communication style. Assertiveness involves expressing one's thoughts, needs, and boundaries in a clear and direct manner while respecting the rights and feelings of others. It is about standing up for oneself without trampling over others.

Women face unique challenges when it comes to assertiveness due to social conditioning and gender expectations. Societal norms often discourage women from being assertive, labeling them as "bossy" or "difficult." However, breaking free from these constraints and embracing assertiveness is essential for women to assert their rights, make their voices heard, and challenge the status quo.

The following chapters will guide you on how to be assertive as a woman. Keep reading!!!

Chapter 1

Understanding Assertiveness

The importance of assertiveness for women in professional and personal contexts.

In today's rapidly evolving world, assertiveness has become a crucial skill for women to navigate both professional and personal realms with confidence and success. By embracing assertiveness, women can overcome barriers, shatter stereotypes, and unleash their true potential.

Understanding Assertiveness
Assertiveness is the art of expressing one's thoughts, needs, and boundaries in a respectful, clear, and confident manner. It involves effectively communicating personal opinions, desires, and rights, while also respecting the rights and opinions of others. It strikes a balance between passive and aggressive

behaviors, allowing women to establish themselves as equals in any setting.

Overcoming gender bias: Assertiveness helps women challenge and overcome gender bias prevalent in professional environments. By confidently voicing their ideas, taking up leadership roles, and negotiating for fair compensation, women can shatter glass ceilings and create a more inclusive workplace culture. Illustration: Imagine a woman confidently leading a team meeting, actively contributing her ideas, and gaining the respect and attention of her colleagues. Her assertiveness helps her break through the gender barriers and be recognized for her skills and expertise.

Effective communication and collaboration: Assertiveness allows women to communicate their thoughts, concerns, and contributions effectively. By expressing themselves clearly and confidently, women can actively participate in decision-making processes, contribute unique perspectives, and build strong professional relationships.

Illustration: Picture a woman engaging in a constructive dialogue with her peers, articulating her viewpoints while actively listening to others. Her assertiveness fosters an environment of open communication and collaboration, enabling her to build strong professional networks and achieve her goals.

Self-advocacy and self-care: Assertiveness empowers women to advocate for their needs and prioritize their well-being. It enables them to set boundaries, say no when necessary, and seek opportunities that align with their values and aspirations.

Illustration: Imagine a woman confidently expressing her preferences and setting boundaries in her personal relationships. Her assertiveness allows her to maintain a healthy work-life balance, prioritize self-care, and nurture fulfilling connections.

Empowering decision-making: Assertiveness equips women with the confidence to make informed decisions aligned with their goals and values. It helps them voice their opinions, ask for support, and take ownership of their choices, fostering personal growth and fulfillment.

Illustration: Visualize a woman assertively asserting her career aspirations, making bold decisions, and taking charge of her professional journey. Her assertiveness empowers her to pursue her passions and reach her full potential.

Assertiveness is an essential trait for women in both professional and personal contexts. By embracing assertiveness, women can break free from societal expectations, challenge stereotypes, and become catalysts for change. It enables women to communicate effectively, navigate obstacles, and achieve their goals while maintaining their dignity and self-respect. Embracing assertiveness is a transformative journey that leads to personal growth, professional success, and a more equal and inclusive society. So, let us celebrate assertiveness as a superpower that every woman can wield to create a brighter and empowered future.

Dispelling Common Misconceptions About Assertiveness.

Assertiveness is often misunderstood, particularly when it comes to women. Misconceptions surrounding assertiveness can hinder women from embracing this empowering trait. We aim to debunk common misconceptions through a relatable life story, shedding light on the true essence and benefits of assertiveness for women.

Embracing Authenticity and Assertiveness

Meet Maya, a talented professional who was often regarded as "too aggressive" when she voiced her opinions in meetings. Frustrated by the misinterpretation of her assertive communication style, Maya sought to dispel the misconceptions surrounding assertiveness.

Misconception 1: Assertiveness equals aggression.

Maya's colleagues often labeled her assertive demeanor as aggressive, assuming she was confrontational and abrasive. However, Maya's assertiveness stemmed from a desire to express herself honestly and effectively. She realized that assertiveness is not about overpowering others but rather about communicating confidently while respecting the thoughts and opinions of others. Maya decided to educate her colleagues about the distinction between assertiveness and aggression through open conversations and by leading by example.

Misconception 2: Assertiveness is a masculine trait.

Maya noticed that some people equated assertiveness with masculinity, believing that women should be passive and accommodating. However, she knew that assertiveness is a universal trait that everyone, regardless of gender, should cultivate. Maya shared her personal journey of embracing assertiveness, emphasizing that it is about self-advocacy, setting boundaries, and standing up for what one believes in. By debunking the notion that assertiveness is exclusive to one gender, Maya encouraged both women and men to embrace their authentic voices.

Misconception 3: Assertiveness hinders likability.

Maya faced the misconception that assertive women are less likable. Some individuals believed that being assertive would make her come across as aggressive and difficult to work with. However, Maya recognized that true assertiveness is about finding a balance between being respectful and expressing oneself. She demonstrated that assertiveness, when coupled with empathy and active listening, enhances collaboration and strengthens relationships. Maya's ability to assertively communicate her ideas while valuing the contributions of others helped her build a reputation as a respected and likable professional.

Maya's story exemplifies the common misconceptions surrounding assertiveness for women. By dispelling these misconceptions, we can empower women to embrace assertiveness authentically. Assertiveness is not aggression but a means to express oneself confidently and respectfully. It is not limited to any gender and can be cultivated by all. Additionally, assertiveness does not hinder likability; on the contrary, it fosters stronger connections and more effective collaboration. By shedding light on these truths, we can pave the way for women to unlock their true potential, communicate assertively, and make their voices heard in both professional and personal contexts. Let us dispel the misconceptions, embrace assertiveness, and create a world where women can thrive and succeed on their own terms

The Benefits of Developing Assertiveness Skills.

Developing assertiveness skills is a powerful journey that equips women with the tools to navigate professional and personal spheres with confidence and effectiveness. We will explore the numerous benefits of cultivating assertiveness skills specifically for women, empowering them to break barriers, shatter stereotypes, and achieve their goals with unwavering conviction.

1: Enhanced Self-Advocacy

1.1 *Increased self-confidence:* Developing assertiveness skills fosters self-assurance, empowering women to believe in their abilities and contributions. Through assertive communication, they become more confident in expressing their ideas, opinions, and aspirations.

Picture a woman confidently presenting her innovative solutions during a team meeting, commanding attention and respect. Her assertiveness not only highlights her competence but also inspires others to recognize her value.

1.2 *Asserting boundaries and needs:* Assertiveness enables women to establish clear boundaries and effectively communicate their needs. By expressing their limits and expectations, women create environments that respect their well-being and ensure equitable treatment.

Imagine a woman assertively setting boundaries with her colleagues, allocating time for personal priorities and self-care. Her assertiveness empowers her to maintain a healthy work-life balance and prioritize her overall wellness.

2: Career Advancement
2.1 Increased professional visibility:
Developing assertiveness skills allows women to be more visible in professional settings. By confidently voicing their accomplishments, sharing their expertise, and actively participating in discussions, they seize opportunities for growth and recognition.

Visualize a woman assertively discussing her achievements during a performance review, showcasing her valuable contributions and positioning herself for career advancement. Her assertiveness amplifies her professional presence and opens doors to new opportunities.

2.2 Effective negotiation and advocacy:
Assertiveness equips women with the ability to negotiate fair compensation, promotions, and opportunities. By asserting their value and advocating for themselves, they break through gender-related barriers and narrow the wage gap.

Picture a woman assertively negotiating a salary increase, armed with market research and a clear understanding of her worth. Her assertiveness empowers her to bridge the pay disparity and achieve equitable compensation.

3: Healthy Relationships and Personal Growth

3.1 Improved interpersonal dynamics:

Developing assertiveness skills strengthens interpersonal relationships by fostering open and honest communication. Women who assert their needs and opinions respectfully cultivate trust, understanding, and deeper connections with others.

Imagine a woman assertively expressing her concerns and expectations to her partner, nurturing a relationship built on mutual respect and shared understanding. Her assertiveness promotes healthy and fulfilling connections.

3.2 Empowered decision-making:

Assertiveness empowers women to make decisions aligned with their values and aspirations. By asserting their choices and desires, they take ownership of their lives, making decisions that align with their authentic selves.

Visualize a woman assertively pursuing her passion and embarking on a new career path, unswayed by societal expectations. Her assertiveness enables her to embrace personal growth and find fulfillment on her own terms.

Developing assertiveness skills is a transformative process that empowers women to navigate professional challenges, build meaningful relationships, and embrace personal growth. By cultivating assertiveness, women unleash their inner strength, influence, and authentic selves. Let us celebrate the benefits of assertiveness, empowering women to overcome obstacles, seize opportunities, and shape a more inclusive and equitable world where their voices are heard and respected.

1.1 Defining Assertiveness

Differentiating Assertiveness From Passivity And Aggression

In the intricate dance of communication, women have often found themselves navigating a delicate balance between assertiveness, passivity, and aggression. Understanding these three distinct behaviors and learning to differentiate them is crucial for women to express their opinions, needs, and boundaries effectively. We will embark on a journey of self-discovery, exploring real-life scenarios that shed light on the subtleties between assertiveness, passivity, and aggression. By the end, you will have a newfound appreciation for assertiveness as a powerful tool for personal growth and effective communication.

The Tale of Sarah: An Unveiling of Perspectives:
Meet Sarah, a vibrant and ambitious professional who has recently joined a dynamic workplace. In her initial days, Sarah found herself grappling with the challenge of asserting herself without being perceived as overly aggressive or passive. Let's explore Sarah's encounters and unravel the layers of assertiveness.

Passivity: The Silent Observer:
Sarah's first few weeks at work were marked by passivity. In team meetings, she often hesitated to voice her opinions, fearing that her ideas might be dismissed or that she would come across as pushy. As a result, she found herself in the role of a silent observer, failing to contribute her unique insights. This passivity limited her growth and hindered her ability to make a meaningful impact.

Aggression: The Volcanic Eruption:
After realizing the limitations of passivity, Sarah swung to the other extreme, adopting an aggressive approach. Frustrated by her lack of visibility, she began dominating conversations, interrupting colleagues, and imposing her ideas forcefully. This sudden burst of aggression alienated her from her team and tarnished her professional relationships. Sarah soon realized that aggression, although seemingly powerful, often leads to negative consequences and inhibits collaboration.

Assertiveness: The Balanced Path:
Recognizing the need for a middle ground, Sarah embarked on a journey to cultivate assertiveness. She discovered that assertiveness is about confidently expressing her thoughts, feelings, and needs while respecting the rights and boundaries of others. It is a skill that can be developed through self-awareness, effective communication techniques, and a genuine desire for collaboration.

Differentiating Assertiveness from Passivity and Aggression:

To better understand the distinctions between assertiveness, passivity, and aggression, let's delve into their defining characteristics:

1. Assertiveness involves expressing oneself clearly, directly, and honestly, while considering the perspectives and feelings of others. It is an empowering approach that allows women to communicate their needs, set boundaries, and negotiate without being submissive or domineering. Assertive individuals display confidence, maintain eye

contact, use assertive body language, and actively listen to others.

2. Passivity often arises from a fear of conflict, rejection, or negative judgment. Passive individuals tend to avoid expressing their thoughts and needs, often yielding to others' demands or opinions. This behavior can lead to suppressed emotions, unfulfilled needs, and a lack of personal growth. Passive individuals may struggle with maintaining eye contact, speak softly, and exhibit submissive body language.

3. Aggression involves forceful and often hostile behavior that disregards the rights and feelings of others. Aggressive individuals tend to dominate conversations, use verbal or physical threats, interrupt others frequently, and exhibit confrontational body language. This approach often stems from a desire to control or overpower others, but it undermines effective communication and damages relationships.

The Power of Assertiveness:
For Sarah, understanding assertiveness became a pivotal moment in her personal and professional growth. As she began practicing assertive communication, she noticed positive transformations in her relationships and self-esteem.

Understanding The Key Elements of Assertive Behavior

Assertiveness is a valuable skill that empowers women to express themselves confidently, set boundaries, and navigate interpersonal relationships with grace and effectiveness. We will delve into the key elements of assertive behavior, equipping you with practical knowledge and examples that will help you harness the power of assertiveness in your personal and professional life.

Clear and Direct Communication:
At the heart of assertiveness lies clear and direct communication. This involves expressing your thoughts, opinions, and needs in a straightforward and unambiguous manner.

Avoiding ambiguity ensures that your message is understood accurately, reducing the chances of misinterpretation or misunderstanding. For instance, instead of saying, "I guess I don't mind," an assertive woman would say, "I have a preference for option A."

Active Listening:
Assertive behavior is not only about expressing yourself but also about actively listening to others. When engaging in conversations, give your full attention to the speaker, maintaining eye contact and providing verbal and non-verbal cues to show that you are genuinely interested in what they have to say. By actively listening, you demonstrate respect and empathy, fostering healthier and more constructive communication.

Respecting Personal Boundaries:
Assertive women understand the importance of setting and respecting personal boundaries. They have a clear understanding of what is acceptable and unacceptable in their relationships and interactions. They assertively communicate their boundaries and expect them

to be honored. For example, if someone constantly crosses a personal boundary, an assertive woman will calmly and firmly communicate her discomfort and expectations.

Self-Confidence and Self-Worth:
Assertiveness is rooted in a strong sense of self-confidence and self-worth. Women who embrace assertiveness recognize their own value and believe in their abilities and opinions. This self-assured mindset allows them to express themselves without seeking constant validation or approval from others. By embracing their worth, assertive women radiate a sense of self-assurance that commands respect and fosters positive relationships.

Constructive Conflict Resolution:
Assertiveness enables women to navigate conflicts in a constructive and respectful manner. Rather than avoiding conflicts or resorting to aggression, assertive women actively engage in conflict resolution by expressing their concerns and actively seeking a mutually beneficial solution. They address conflicts directly, focusing on the issue at hand

rather than attacking the person involved. This approach fosters open dialogue and collaborative problem-solving.

Emotional Intelligence:
Assertiveness is closely tied to emotional intelligence, which involves recognizing, understanding, and managing one's own emotions and those of others. Assertive women have a heightened awareness of their emotions, allowing them to express themselves authentically while remaining considerate of others' feelings. By embracing emotional intelligence, they can navigate difficult conversations and challenging situations with empathy and compassion.

Examples of Assertive Behavior:
To illustrate the key elements of assertive behavior, let's consider a few examples:

Scenario: A colleague consistently takes credit for your ideas during team meetings.
Passive response: Stay silent and allow the colleague to continue taking credit.

Aggressive response: Confront the colleague publicly, criticizing their behavior.
Assertive response: Privately approach the colleague, express your concerns, and request that they acknowledge your contributions.

A friend constantly cancels plans at the last minute without valid reasons.
Passive response: Accept the cancellations without expressing your disappointment.
Aggressive response: React angrily and accuse your friend of being inconsiderate.
Assertive response: Communicate calmly but assertively, expressing how their cancellations affect your feelings and suggesting finding a solution that works for both of you.

By understanding and embracing the key elements of assertive behavior, women can unlock their true potential and navigate interpersonal dynamics with confidence and effectiveness. Clear and direct communication, active listening, respecting personal boundaries, self-confidence and self-worth, constructive conflict resolution, and emotional intelligence are the building blocks of assertiveness.

When women embody assertiveness, they experience numerous benefits. They are more likely to have their opinions and needs acknowledged and respected, leading to increased self-esteem and self-respect. Assertive women are also better equipped to handle conflicts and assert their rights without resorting to aggression or passivity. Additionally, assertiveness fosters healthy relationships based on open communication, trust, and mutual understanding.

Developing assertiveness is a journey that requires self-awareness and practice. Here are a few strategies to cultivate assertive behavior:

Self-reflection: Take time to reflect on your values, needs, and boundaries. Identify areas where you tend to be passive or aggressive and explore the underlying reasons for these patterns.

Role-playing: Engage in role-playing exercises with a trusted friend or mentor. Practice expressing your thoughts, needs, and boundaries in assertive ways, simulating real-life situations.

Assertive body language: Pay attention to your body language. Maintain eye contact, stand or sit upright, and use confident and calm gestures. Assertive body language reinforces your message.

"I" statements: Use "I" statements to express your feelings and needs without blaming or attacking others. For example, say, "I feel frustrated when..." instead of "You always..."

Practice active listening: Demonstrate active listening by paraphrasing, asking clarifying questions, and validating others' perspectives. This fosters understanding and builds rapport.

Remember, assertiveness is not about being aggressive or dominating others. It's about expressing yourself confidently while respecting the rights and boundaries of others. It is a skill that can be honed over time, leading to personal growth, enhanced communication, and stronger relationships.

Embrace the power of assertiveness, and let your voice be heard, your needs be met, and your boundaries be respected. You have the ability to navigate life's challenges with grace and confidence, creating a more fulfilling and empowered existence.

Recognizing the Impact of Cultural and Societal Expectations on Women's Assertiveness

Assertiveness is a powerful tool for women to express themselves confidently and navigate various aspects of life. However, cultural and societal expectations often shape and influence women's assertiveness in significant ways. We will explore how cultural and societal norms impact women's assertiveness, shedding light on the challenges they face and providing real-life examples that highlight the complexity of this issue. By understanding these influences, we can work towards creating a more supportive and inclusive environment for women to embrace assertiveness.

Gender Stereotypes and Expectations:
Cultural and societal norms often impose rigid gender stereotypes and expectations, creating barriers for women to assert themselves. For instance, women may be expected to prioritize nurturing and caretaking roles, leading to the perception that assertiveness is contrary to feminine traits. This expectation can result in women feeling pressured to adopt more passive or accommodating behaviors, inhibiting their ability to express their needs and opinions assertively.

Example: In a professional setting, a woman may find herself navigating the stereotype that assertiveness is synonymous with aggressiveness. As a result, she may hesitate to assert her ideas and may feel compelled to downplay her achievements to avoid being perceived as overly assertive or intimidating.

Cultural Values and Power Dynamics:
Cultural values and power dynamics influence women's assertiveness differently across societies. In some cultures, hierarchical structures and traditional gender roles may discourage women from challenging authority or speaking up. This can create a significant barrier to assertiveness, as women may fear backlash or social repercussions.

Example: In certain cultures, women may face cultural expectations that dictate they should defer to male family members or elders in decision-making. This cultural norm can limit their ability to assert themselves in personal and professional contexts, leading to the suppression of their needs and desires.

Perceived Likeability and Social Consequences:
Women often grapple with the perceived trade-off between assertiveness and likeability. Studies have shown that assertive women may face social backlash, including being labeled as "bossy" or "aggressive." The fear of being negatively perceived or facing social

consequences can deter women from asserting themselves fully.

Example: A woman expressing her opinion assertively in a group discussion may be met with dismissive responses or judgment from others. The fear of facing criticism or being ostracized may discourage her from further asserting her ideas, leading to self-doubt and a diminished sense of agency.

Intersectionality and Multiple Identities:
It is essential to recognize that the impact of cultural and societal expectations on assertiveness is intersectional, influenced by factors such as race, ethnicity, socio-economic status, and more. Women from marginalized communities may face additional layers of discrimination and stereotypes that intersect with gender expectations, further complicating their ability to assert themselves.

Example: A woman from an ethnic minority background may encounter stereotypes that label her as submissive or passive. These stereotypes can intersect with gender expectations, making it more challenging for her to assert herself authentically in various settings.

Overcoming Cultural and Societal Barriers:

Recognizing and addressing the impact of cultural and societal expectations on women's assertiveness is crucial for fostering an inclusive and supportive environment. Here are a few strategies to promote assertiveness:

Education and Awareness:

Educate society about the importance of assertiveness and challenge gender stereotypes that limit women's expression. By raising awareness, we can dismantle harmful narratives and encourage a more inclusive understanding of assertive behavior.

Empowerment and Skill-Building:

Offer workshops, training, and resources that focus on building assertiveness skills for women. Providing practical tools and support can empower women to navigate cultural and societal expectations while staying true to their authentic selves.

Role Models and Representation:

Highlight and amplify the voices of assertive women from diverse backgrounds as role models. By showcasing their experiences and successes, we can challenge stereotypes and inspire other women to embrace assertiveness without fear of judgment or backlash.

Creating Supportive Spaces:

Foster inclusive environments that encourage open dialogue and respectful communication. Organizations and communities can establish policies and norms that promote assertiveness, ensuring that women's voices are valued and heard without facing negative consequences.

Challenging Biases and Stereotypes:

Encourage critical thinking and reflection on gender biases and stereotypes. By questioning and challenging these ingrained beliefs, we can create a more inclusive society that recognizes and celebrates the assertiveness of women.

Intersectional Approaches:
Recognize the unique challenges faced by women from different cultural, racial, and socio-economic backgrounds. Adopt an intersectional lens that acknowledges the overlapping systems of oppression and works towards dismantling these barriers to assertiveness.

The impact of cultural and societal expectations on women's assertiveness is significant and multifaceted. By understanding these influences, we can collectively work towards creating a more supportive and inclusive environment. Through education, empowerment, representation, and challenging biases, we can create spaces where women feel empowered to assert themselves authentically, express their needs and opinions confidently, and contribute fully to all aspects of life. Embracing assertiveness as a fundamental right for all women is a crucial step towards equality, personal growth, and positive social change.

1.2 The Role of Assertiveness in Professional Success:

In today's dynamic and competitive professional landscape, women have made significant strides towards achieving equality and recognition. However, they still encounter unique challenges that require the cultivation of essential skills. One such skill is assertiveness, which plays a pivotal role in the professional success of women. We will explore the importance of assertiveness and how it empowers women to excel in their careers.

Understanding Assertiveness:
Assertiveness is a communication style characterized by the ability to express thoughts, needs, and opinions confidently and respectfully, while also considering the rights and feelings of others. It is about striking a balance between passivity and aggression, promoting effective collaboration and healthy boundaries.

Building Self-Confidence:

Assertiveness starts with a strong foundation of self-confidence. By embracing assertiveness, women can overcome self-doubt and develop a positive self-image. Confidence enables women to articulate their ideas and ambitions, stand up for themselves, and take calculated risks, leading to increased visibility and opportunities in the professional arena.

Effective Communication:

Assertiveness empowers women to communicate their thoughts and ideas clearly, directly, and with conviction. By expressing themselves assertively, women can effectively navigate workplace dynamics, engage in constructive dialogue, and influence decision-making processes. Clear and confident communication establishes credibility and fosters respect among colleagues, superiors, and clients.

Setting Boundaries:

In professional settings, women often face challenges related to workload, work-life balance, and assertively asserting their boundaries. By embracing assertiveness, women can clearly articulate their limits, negotiate reasonable expectations, and advocate for themselves without compromising their well-being. Setting boundaries not only promotes personal growth but also establishes a framework for success, ensuring that women's professional contributions are valued and recognized.

Conflict Resolution:
Conflicts are an inevitable part of any workplace environment. Assertive women are equipped with the skills to navigate conflicts constructively, addressing issues head-on while maintaining professionalism and respect. By expressing their needs and concerns assertively, women can find collaborative solutions and foster a positive work environment conducive to productivity and growth.

Leadership Development:
Assertiveness is a key trait of successful leaders. Women who embrace assertiveness position themselves as capable leaders, inspiring and motivating their teams towards shared goals.

By confidently expressing their vision, delegating tasks, and providing constructive feedback, assertive women cultivate an environment that encourages creativity, innovation, and inclusivity.

Networking and Career Advancement:
Assertiveness is instrumental in networking and seizing career advancement opportunities. Women who assertively promote their achievements, engage in meaningful conversations, and build professional relationships establish a strong personal brand and expand their influence within their industry. Assertive women are more likely to be considered for promotions, challenging assignments, and leadership roles, propelling their professional growth.

In the pursuit of professional success, assertiveness is an indispensable skill for women. By embracing assertiveness, women can build self-confidence, enhance communication skills, set boundaries, resolve conflicts, develop leadership abilities, and leverage networking opportunities. It empowers women to overcome barriers, shatter glass ceilings, and leave an indelible mark in their chosen fields. The role of assertiveness in the professional success of women cannot be overstated, as it fosters an environment of equality, respect, and inclusion, benefiting individuals and organizations alike.

Exploring the Link Between Assertiveness and Career Advancement.

In today's fast-paced and competitive professional world, the link between assertiveness and career advancement in women is gaining recognition. Assertiveness, as a crucial skill, can significantly influence a woman's trajectory in her chosen field. We will delve into the connection between assertiveness and career advancement, highlighting how cultivating assertiveness can propel women towards greater success.

Understanding Assertiveness:
Assertiveness is the ability to express oneself confidently and effectively, while respecting the rights and opinions of others. It involves clear

communication, setting boundaries, and advocating for one's needs in a professional manner. An assertive woman possesses the ability to assert herself while maintaining a balance between aggression and passivity.

The Impact of Assertiveness on Career Advancement:

Increased Visibility:

Assertiveness enables women to make their presence known in the workplace. By actively voicing their opinions, ideas, and accomplishments, assertive women grab the attention of their colleagues, superiors, and decision-makers. Their contributions are recognized, leading to increased visibility and opportunities for advancement.

For example, imagine a team meeting where an assertive woman confidently presents a well-researched idea. Her assertive communication style grabs the attention of senior management, who appreciate her ability to articulate her thoughts clearly. As a result, she is given the opportunity to lead the implementation of the project, propelling her career forward.

Enhanced Leadership Skills: Assertive women often display strong leadership qualities. Their ability to communicate assertively empowers them to effectively lead teams, delegate tasks, and provide constructive feedback. By demonstrating assertiveness in leadership positions, women position themselves as capable and influential leaders, opening doors to further career advancement.
For instance, consider a scenario where a team encounters a conflict. An assertive female leader steps in, facilitates open communication, and works towards a resolution. Her assertiveness in addressing the issue constructively not only resolves the conflict but also earns her respect and admiration from her team and superiors, setting her up for future leadership roles.

Negotiation and Career Progression: Assertiveness plays a vital role in negotiation, a skill essential for career advancement. Women who assertively negotiate their salaries, benefits, and career opportunities can secure more favorable terms. By valuing their worth and advocating for themselves, they establish a foundation for continued success and advancement.

For example, an assertive woman who confidently negotiates a higher salary based on her expertise and achievements sends a clear message about her value to the organization. This not only improves her financial prospects but also positions her for future growth and recognition.

Networking and Relationship Building: Assertive women actively engage in networking, forming valuable professional relationships that contribute to their career advancement. By confidently expressing their ideas, sharing their accomplishments, and seeking opportunities to collaborate, assertive women build strong networks that open doors to new opportunities and career growth.

Consider a networking event where an assertive woman approaches industry leaders, confidently initiating conversations and showcasing her expertise. By assertively promoting herself and fostering connections, she expands her professional network, opening doors to career-enhancing collaborations, mentorship, and referrals.

Assertiveness is a powerful tool that can significantly impact a woman's career advancement. By cultivating assertiveness, women can increase their visibility, enhance their leadership skills, negotiate more effectively, and build strong professional networks. The ability to assert oneself confidently and professionally paves the way for greater opportunities and recognition. Embracing assertiveness not only benefits individual women but also contributes to the broader goal of achieving gender equality and empowering women in the professional sphere.

Overcoming Gender-Related Challenges in the Workplace.

In today's modern society, women continue to face unique challenges in the workplace due to gender-related biases and stereotypes. Overcoming these obstacles requires resilience, determination, and a proactive approach. We will explore the journey of a woman named Maya, highlighting the gender-related challenges she encountered and the strategies she employed to overcome them, inspiring other women to navigate their own paths to success.

Maya's Story: A Journey of Triumph over Gender Bias

Meet Maya, a talented and ambitious professional who embarked on her career with great enthusiasm. However, she soon discovered that gender-related challenges awaited her at every turn.

Breaking Stereotypes:
Maya realized that traditional gender stereotypes were holding her back. Instead of being discouraged, she decided to challenge these stereotypes by showcasing her skills and capabilities. Maya actively sought out opportunities to demonstrate her expertise, proving that she could excel in traditionally male-dominated fields.

For instance, when she joined a technology company, Maya noticed that women were often overlooked for technical roles. Determined to break the stereotype, she took the initiative to participate in coding competitions and consistently delivered exceptional results. Her efforts shattered preconceived notions, earning her the respect and recognition she deserved.

Building Supportive Networks:
Recognizing the power of networking, Maya sought out other professional women who faced similar challenges. She joined women-centric organizations, attended conferences, and actively engaged in mentorship programs. By surrounding herself with like-minded individuals, Maya found a supportive community that provided valuable guidance, encouragement, and opportunities.

One such instance involved a networking event where Maya met a successful female executive who had overcome gender barriers herself. Impressed by Maya's drive and potential, the executive became her mentor, offering advice, advocating for her, and introducing her to influential contacts. With the support of her network, Maya gained the confidence to navigate the workplace more effectively.

Assertiveness and Negotiation:

Maya realized that being assertive and adept at negotiation was crucial in overcoming gender-related challenges. She actively worked on honing her communication skills, finding her voice, and advocating for herself and her accomplishments. Maya developed a clear understanding of her worth and did not shy away from negotiating for fair compensation, promotions, and opportunities.

An example of Maya's assertiveness was when she approached her manager for a promotion after consistently exceeding expectations. She presented a well-prepared case, highlighting her achievements and the value she brought to the organization. Through her assertive approach, Maya not only secured the promotion but also gained respect and recognition for her capabilities.

Continuous Learning and Skill Development:

Maya recognized the importance of continuous learning and skill development in overcoming gender-related challenges. She proactively sought out training programs, workshops, and educational opportunities to enhance her knowledge and stay ahead in her field. Maya understood that by constantly improving herself, she could not only counter gender biases but also position herself as a valuable asset to any organization.

For instance, when Maya encountered gender-related biases during a team project, she invested time in learning about diversity and inclusion initiatives. Armed with this knowledge, she organized a workshop for her team, promoting a culture of inclusivity and understanding. Her proactive approach not only fostered a more inclusive work environment but also garnered recognition for her leadership abilities.

Maya's journey serves as an inspiration for women facing gender-related challenges in the workplace. By challenging stereotypes, building supportive networks, practicing assertiveness and negotiation, and investing in continuous learning, women can overcome these obstacles and thrive in their careers. Maya's story highlights the importance of resilience, determination, and empowerment in navigating gender biases, ultimately paving the way for greater gender equality and inclusivity in the professional world.

Case Studies Highlighting Successful Assertive Women in Various Industries

Assertiveness is a powerful quality that empowers women to succeed in various industries. We will explore inspiring case studies of successful assertive women who have made significant strides in their respective fields. These examples serve as a testament to the transformative power of assertiveness and provide valuable insights into how it can contribute to professional success.

Sheryl Sandberg - Technology Industry
Sheryl Sandberg, the Chief Operating Officer of Facebook, is renowned for her assertive

leadership style and advocacy for women in the workplace. Throughout her career, Sandberg fearlessly voiced her opinions and championed gender equality initiatives. Her bestselling book, "Lean In," inspired women to embrace their ambitions and assertively pursue leadership positions. Sandberg's assertiveness and dedication to empowering women have made her an influential figure in the technology industry.

Indra Nooyi - Business and Leadership
Indra Nooyi, former CEO of PepsiCo, is an exceptional example of an assertive woman who achieved remarkable success in the business world. Nooyi demonstrated assertiveness by reshaping PepsiCo's product portfolio to focus on healthier options, even in the face of initial resistance. She confidently led the company through challenging times, establishing herself as a visionary leader. Nooyi's assertiveness, strategic thinking, and commitment to innovation propelled her to the top of her industry.

Mary Barra - Automotive Industry

Mary Barra, the Chairwoman and CEO of General Motors, is a trailblazer in the traditionally male-dominated automotive industry. Known for her assertive leadership style, Barra has implemented bold changes to position General Motors as a leader in electric and autonomous vehicles. Her ability to assertively communicate her vision and make tough decisions has been pivotal in driving the company's growth and success. Barra's accomplishments highlight the transformative impact of assertiveness in breaking barriers and leading with conviction.

Serena Williams - Sports and Advocacy

Serena Williams, one of the greatest tennis players of all time, exemplifies assertiveness both on and off the court. Known for her fierce determination and unwavering confidence, Williams has shattered numerous records and faced adversity with resilience. Beyond her athletic achievements, Williams uses her platform to advocate for gender and racial equality. Her assertiveness in speaking out against injustice and fighting for equal treatment has made her an icon of empowerment in the sports industry.

Ruth Bader Ginsburg - Legal and Judicial System

Ruth Bader Ginsburg, an associate justice of the Supreme Court of the United States, was a pioneering force in advocating for gender equality and women's rights. Throughout her career, Ginsburg fearlessly fought against gender-based discrimination and consistently asserted her positions on key legal issues. Her unwavering assertiveness and dedication to justice have left a lasting impact on the legal and judicial system, inspiring generations of women to assert their rights and pursue careers in law.

These case studies demonstrate the immense impact of assertiveness in empowering women across various industries. Sheryl Sandberg, Indra Nooyi, Mary Barra, Serena Williams, and Ruth Bader Ginsburg have blazed trails through their unwavering confidence, strong leadership, and advocacy. By embracing assertiveness, women can overcome barriers, challenge stereotypes, and achieve remarkable success. These remarkable women serve as role models, showcasing the transformative power of assertiveness in driving change and shaping the future of their industries.

Chapter 2:

Building Self-Confidence

The connection between self-confidence and assertiveness.

In today's ever-evolving society, empowering women to embrace their true potential is an essential goal. Two crucial elements that contribute to a woman's personal growth and success are self-confidence and assertiveness. These qualities go hand in hand, intertwining to create a powerful combination that enables women to thrive in various aspects of life.

Understanding Self-Confidence:
Self-confidence forms the foundation upon which assertiveness is built. It refers to a woman's belief in her abilities, skills, and intrinsic worth. A strong sense of self-confidence allows women to tackle challenges head-on, take risks, and pursue their goals with determination. Self-confident

women embrace their strengths while acknowledging areas for improvement, leading to personal growth and increased resilience.

Case Study: Sarah's Journey to Self-Confidence
Sarah, a professional in her late twenties, initially struggled with low self-confidence. Through self-reflection and personal development, she gradually built her self-esteem. As her self-confidence grew, Sarah found herself more willing to express her opinions, stand up for her ideas in team meetings, and take on leadership roles. Her assertiveness at work not only enhanced her professional reputation but also fostered positive relationships with colleagues and superiors.

Unleashing Assertiveness:
Assertiveness is the ability to communicate and express oneself confidently, respecting one's own needs and boundaries while considering others'. Assertive women effectively voice their opinions, assert their rights, and negotiate with clarity and conviction. This skill empowers women to establish healthy boundaries,

advocate for themselves, and navigate challenging situations effectively.

Case Study: Maya's Journey to Assertiveness

Maya, a young entrepreneur, recognized her innate potential but struggled with asserting herself in business negotiations. Through assertiveness training, she learned to express her needs and negotiate favorable terms without compromising her values. Maya's newfound assertiveness not only boosted her business ventures but also positively impacted her personal relationships. By speaking up and asserting herself, she gained respect and admiration from her peers.

The Synergistic Connection:

Self-confidence and assertiveness form a powerful synergy that propels women towards success. When women possess both qualities, they experience a transformation in various areas of life, including personal relationships, career growth, and personal well-being.

Case Study: Emma's Transformation through Self-Confidence and Assertiveness

Emma, a recent college graduate, embarked on a journey of self-discovery to overcome her self-doubt and passivity. As she developed her self-confidence and assertiveness, Emma started setting clear boundaries with friends and family, prioritizing her own needs. She also confidently pursued job opportunities aligned with her passions and skills. The combination of self-confidence and assertiveness propelled Emma to make bold decisions, leading to increased happiness and fulfillment in her personal and professional life.

The connection between self-confidence and assertiveness in women is undeniably powerful and transformative. Self-confidence provides the necessary belief in one's abilities, while assertiveness allows for effective communication and the assertion of one's needs. Through real-life case studies, we have witnessed the empowering impact of this combination on women's personal growth, career advancement, and overall well-being. By nurturing self-confidence and cultivating assertiveness, women can embrace their full potential and contribute to a more inclusive and empowering society.

Identifying personal barriers to self-confidence

Self-confidence is a vital attribute that empowers women to navigate life's challenges with resilience and conviction. However, numerous personal barriers can hinder the development of self-confidence, preventing women from fully embracing their potential.

Negative Self-Talk and Limiting Beliefs:
One significant barrier to self-confidence is negative self-talk and limiting beliefs. These internal narratives often stem from societal expectations, past experiences, or comparison with others. Negative self-talk reinforces self-doubt and undermines a woman's belief in her abilities, inhibiting her from pursuing her goals and taking risks.

Mia's Battle with Negative Self-Talk

Mia, a talented artist, constantly compared herself to others in her field, leading to self-doubt and diminished confidence in her own abilities. Through self-reflection and therapy, Mia learned to challenge her negative self-talk and reframe her limiting beliefs. By cultivating self-compassion and focusing on her unique strengths, she gradually dismantled the barriers that had held her back, ultimately gaining the confidence to showcase her artwork and pursue her passion wholeheartedly.

Fear of Failure and Perfectionism:
The fear of failure and perfectionism can cripple a woman's self-confidence. The desire to achieve flawlessness and avoid making mistakes can create undue pressure and paralyze one's progress. Perfectionism often leads to setting unattainable standards, causing women to doubt their abilities and fear taking necessary risks.

Olivia's Struggle with Perfectionism

Olivia, a high-achieving student, constantly sought perfection in her academic pursuits. This quest for flawlessness created immense anxiety and self-doubt, hindering her overall self-confidence. Through therapy and self-reflection, Olivia recognized the importance of embracing imperfections as learning opportunities. She gradually shifted her focus from outcomes to personal growth, allowing herself to take risks and make mistakes. As a result, Olivia's self-confidence flourished, and she achieved success while maintaining a healthy balance in her life.

External Validation and Comparison:
Relying on external validation and constant comparison to others is a significant barrier to self-confidence. Seeking approval from others for self-worth places one's confidence in the hands of others, making it fragile and susceptible to fluctuations. Constant comparison erodes self-esteem, as women often perceive themselves as falling short in comparison to unrealistic standards set by society or peers.

Lily's Journey to Self-Acceptance

Lily, a young professional, struggled with seeking validation from her colleagues and constantly comparing herself to her accomplished peers. This behavior took a toll on her self-confidence and hindered her professional growth. Through introspection and self-care practices, Lily realized the importance of self-acceptance and embracing her unique journey. By shifting her focus inward and celebrating her own achievements, she broke free from the chains of external validation, nurturing her self-confidence and allowing it to thrive.

Understanding and identifying personal barriers to self-confidence is crucial for women seeking to unleash their true potential. By recognizing the detrimental impact of negative self-talk, fear of failure, perfectionism, and external validation, women can embark on a journey of self-discovery and growth. Through relatable case studies, we have witnessed how confronting and overcoming these barriers leads to enhanced self-confidence. With self-compassion, self-acceptance, and a commitment to personal growth, women can break free from these obstacles and embrace their authentic selves with unwavering confidence.

Cultivating a positive mindset for assertiveness

Assertiveness is a powerful tool that allows women to confidently express their needs, opinions, and boundaries while respecting those of others. To cultivate assertiveness, it is essential to nurture a positive mindset that supports self-belief, self-empowerment, and effective communication.

Embracing Self-Affirmation and Positive Self-Talk:

A positive mindset begins with self-affirmation and positive self-talk. Self-affirmation involves consciously recognizing and appreciating one's strengths, accomplishments, and unique qualities. Positive self-talk entails replacing self-criticism with kind and empowering inner dialogue.

Encouraging Self-Affirmation: Women can create a daily practice of acknowledging their achievements, affirming their worth, and celebrating their strengths. By internalizing positive beliefs about themselves, women can cultivate a strong foundation for assertiveness.

Harnessing Positive Self-Talk: Women can consciously challenge negative thoughts and replace them with affirming and supportive self-talk. By reframing self-doubt into self-encouragement, women can enhance their belief in their capabilities, fostering assertiveness.

Fostering a Growth Mindset:
A growth mindset is the belief that abilities and intelligence can be developed through dedication and effort. Embracing a growth mindset helps women view challenges as opportunities for growth rather than obstacles. This perspective encourages resilience and a willingness to take risks.

Embracing Challenges: Women can approach challenging situations with curiosity and a desire to learn. Instead of fearing failure, they can perceive it as a stepping stone to personal development, building their assertiveness along the way.

Learning from Setbacks: Adopting a growth mindset enables women to view setbacks as temporary and learning experiences. By analyzing their mistakes and extracting valuable lessons, they can bounce back stronger and more assertive in subsequent endeavors.

Building Self-Confidence through Competence:
Competence in a particular skill or area breeds self-confidence, facilitating assertiveness. By continuously developing their knowledge and abilities, women can reinforce their belief in themselves and their capacity to excel.
Identifying Skill Gaps: Women can assess areas where they feel less confident and actively seek opportunities for growth and learning. Whether through formal education, mentorship, or self-study, acquiring new skills enhances self-confidence and assertiveness.

Celebrating Achievements: Recognizing and celebrating personal milestones and achievements boosts self-confidence. By acknowledging progress and successes, women reinforce their belief in their abilities, fueling assertiveness in various aspects of life.

Cultivating a positive mindset is a powerful catalyst for assertiveness in women. By embracing self-affirmation, positive self-talk, and a growth mindset, women can overcome self-doubt, fear, and societal conditioning that may hinder their assertive expression. Fostering competence and celebrating achievements further solidifies their self-confidence, allowing them to navigate challenges with poise and effective communication. Through these strategies, women can cultivate a positive mindset that empowers them to embrace their assertiveness, unlocking their full potential and fostering personal and professional fulfillment.

2.1 Embracing Self-Acceptance:

Developing a healthy self image and embracing strengths as women

In a world that constantly bombards women with unrealistic beauty standards and societal expectations, it is crucial to develop a healthy self-image and embrace our strengths. By cultivating a positive mindset and recognizing our unique qualities, we empower ourselves to thrive and make a lasting impact.

Understanding Self-Image:

Self-image refers to how we perceive ourselves, encompassing our thoughts, beliefs, and feelings about our own identity. It influences our confidence, behavior, and interactions with the world. Developing a healthy self-image involves recognizing and appreciating our individuality, including our physical appearance, abilities, and character traits.

Challenging Unrealistic Standards:

Society often imposes narrow beauty standards that can negatively impact women's self-esteem. It is vital to challenge these unrealistic expectations and remember that true beauty comes in all shapes, sizes, and colors. By embracing our unique features and celebrating diversity, we can foster a positive self-image and inspire others to do the same.

Cultivating Self-Compassion:

Self-compassion is the practice of treating ourselves with kindness, understanding, and acceptance. Instead of dwelling on perceived flaws or failures, we should embrace self-compassion as a powerful tool for personal growth. By offering ourselves empathy and forgiveness, we create a nurturing environment for self-improvement and build a stronger sense of self.

Identifying Strengths:

Every woman possesses an array of strengths, talents, and abilities. Identifying and embracing these strengths is crucial for developing a healthy self-image. Reflect on your accomplishments, skills, and passions. Recognize the unique qualities that make you stand out and appreciate the value they bring to your life and the world around you.

Setting Realistic Goals:

Setting realistic goals allows us to focus on personal growth while maintaining a healthy perspective. By defining achievable objectives, we set ourselves up for success and boost our confidence. Break down bigger goals into smaller, manageable steps, and celebrate each milestone along the way. This approach encourages a positive self-image and reinforces the belief in our capabilities.

Building a Supportive Network:
Surrounding ourselves with a supportive network of family, friends, and mentors plays a vital role in developing a healthy self-image. Seek out individuals who uplift and encourage you to embrace your strengths. Engage in meaningful conversations, share experiences, and learn from one another. By building a strong support system, we can nurture our self-esteem and continue to grow.

Practicing Self-Care:
Self-care is a fundamental aspect of developing a healthy self-image. Prioritize activities that promote your physical, emotional, and mental well-being. Engage in regular exercise, maintain a balanced diet, practice mindfulness, and allocate time for hobbies and relaxation. By investing in self-care, you demonstrate self-worth and reinforce a positive self-image.

Embracing Growth and Learning:
Embracing a growth mindset allows us to view challenges as opportunities for growth and development. Recognize that setbacks and failures are part of the journey and use them as

stepping stones towards personal improvement. Embrace new experiences, expand your knowledge, and seek out opportunities for self-discovery. This continuous learning mindset enables you to unlock your full potential and reinforces a healthy self-image.

Developing a healthy self-image and embracing strengths as women is a lifelong journey that requires self-reflection, self-compassion, and a supportive network. By challenging societal expectations, recognizing our unique qualities, setting realistic goals, and practicing self-care, we empower ourselves to thrive. Let us embrace our strengths, uplift one another, and inspire future generations of women to

Overcoming self-doubt and imposter syndrome in women

Self-doubt and imposter syndrome are common hurdles that many women face on their professional and personal journeys. These negative feelings can undermine confidence, hinder progress, and prevent us from realizing our full potential. However, by understanding the roots of self-doubt and imposter syndrome and employing effective strategies, we can overcome these obstacles and cultivate a strong sense of self-assurance.

Understanding Self-Doubt and Imposter Syndrome:

Self-doubt is the lack of confidence in one's abilities or worth, while imposter syndrome is the persistent fear of being exposed as a fraud despite evidence of competence. These feelings often stem from perfectionism, comparison to others, and societal pressures. Recognizing that self-doubt and imposter syndrome are common experiences can be the first step towards overcoming them.

Sarah, an accomplished marketing professional, often doubts her skills and achievements, attributing her success to luck rather than her own abilities. She constantly fears that others will discover she is not as competent as they believe.

Celebrating Achievements and Acknowledging Strengths:

Acknowledge your accomplishments, both big and small, and celebrate them. Reflect on the skills, knowledge, and experiences that have contributed to your success. Recognizing your strengths and reminding yourself of past achievements can boost confidence and counteract self-doubt.

Amelia, a talented graphic designer, starts a journal where she writes down her achievements, positive feedback from clients, and milestones she has reached. When self-doubt arises, she reads through her journal, reminding herself of her capabilities and the impact she has made.

Challenging Negative Self-Talk:

Negative self-talk is a destructive pattern that fuels self-doubt and imposter syndrome. Challenge the negative thoughts and replace them with positive and affirming statements. Practice self-compassion and treat yourself with the same kindness and encouragement you would offer a frien

Maria, a software engineer, catches herself thinking, "I don't deserve this promotion; I'm not skilled enough." She consciously reframes her thoughts, saying, "I have worked hard to acquire the necessary skills, and my accomplishments speak for themselves. I am deserving of this promotion."

Seeking Support and Mentorship:
Reach out to a supportive network of friends, family, or mentors who can provide guidance and encouragement. Discuss your feelings of self-doubt and imposter syndrome openly, as sharing your experiences can help alleviate their weight and provide valuable perspectives.
Lisa, a young entrepreneur, joins a professional networking group where she meets experienced women who have faced similar challenges. Through their shared stories and advice, she gains support and inspiration, which bolsters her confidence and helps her overcome self-doubt.

Embracing Failure and Learning Opportunities:

View failures and setbacks as opportunities for growth and learning rather than as proof of incompetence. Embrace a growth mindset and understand that setbacks are a natural part of any journey. Extract valuable lessons from failures and use them as stepping stones to future success.

Example:

Emma, a scientist, experiences a setback in her research project. Instead of succumbing to self-doubt, she analyzes the situation objectively, identifies areas for improvement, and views the setback as a chance to refine her approach and make her work even stronger.

Cultivating Self-Confidence Through Preparation:

Preparation plays a crucial role in building self-confidence. Invest time and effort into honing your skills, expanding your knowledge, and staying up-to-date in your field. The more prepared you feel, the less room

Utilizing affirmations and visualization techniques

Affirmations and visualization techniques are powerful tools that can empower women to overcome obstacles, build self-confidence, and achieve their goals. By harnessing the positive energy of affirmations and engaging in vivid visualizations, women can cultivate a mindset of success and manifest their dreams into reality.

Affirmations: Shaping Positive Self-Talk

Affirmations are positive statements that assert desired qualities, beliefs, or outcomes. By consciously shaping our self-talk, we can reprogram negative thought patterns and replace them with empowering affirmations. Affirmations help to build self-confidence, boost motivation, and foster a positive mindset.

Visualization: Creating a Clear Mental Picture

Visualization involves creating vivid mental images of desired outcomes and experiences. By visualizing ourselves achieving our goals, we tap into the power of the subconscious mind, which can pave the way for actualizing our aspirations. Visualization enhances focus, motivation, and confidence.

Combining Affirmations and Visualization:

When affirmations and visualization techniques are combined, they create a potent synergy. Affirmations provide the positive mindset and belief system, while visualization adds depth and sensory details to the mental picture, making it more vivid and compelling.

Sophie, a public speaker, utilizes both affirmations and visualization techniques. Before stepping on stage, she affirms, "I am a captivating speaker who engages and inspires my audience." She then visualizes herself confidently delivering her speech, making eye contact, and receiving enthusiastic applause. This combined approach enhances her self-assurance and sets the stage for a successful presentation.

Creating Affirmations and Visualizations:

When crafting affirmations and visualizations, consider the following guidelines:

Be Specific: State your affirmations and visualizations with clarity, specifying the desired outcome or trait you wish to embody.

Use Positive Language: Frame your affirmations and visualizations in positive terms, focusing on what you want to achieve or experience rather than what you want to avoid.

Engage Your Emotions: Attach strong positive emotions to your affirmations and visualizations, as emotions fuel the manifestation process and increase motivation.

Be Realistic yet Ambitious: Set affirmations and visualizations that are challenging but attainable, stretching your capabilities while maintaining a sense of belief in their achievement.

Example:

Laura, a budding writer, crafts her affirmation: "I am a successful and published author, captivating readers with my words." She visualizes herself holding her published book, feeling the satisfaction of seeing her words in print, and receiving positive reviews. This affirmation and visualization combination energizes her writing journey and fuels her determination.

Consistency and Repetition:
Consistency is key when utilizing affirmations and visualization techniques. Make them a part of your daily routine, incorporating them into your morning rituals or meditation practices. Repetition helps to rewire the subconscious mind, reinforcing positive beliefs and strengthening the manifestation process.

2.2 Setting Realistic Goals

Defining short-term and long-term goals

For women, cultivating assertiveness skills can be particularly transformative, enabling them to overcome societal barriers and reach new heights of success. We will delve into the significance of defining short-term and long-term goals in assertiveness as a woman.

I. Short-term Goals: Building a Foundation for Assertiveness

Enhancing Self-Awareness:
Short-term goals in assertiveness often begin with developing a deep understanding of oneself. This involves identifying personal strengths, weaknesses, values, and beliefs. For instance, a woman might set a short-term goal to recognize her communication style and become aware of any self-limiting beliefs or behaviors that hinder her assertiveness.

Assertive Communication Skills:
Effective communication is crucial for assertiveness. Setting short-term goals to improve communication skills can include learning active listening techniques, practicing clear and concise self-expression, and acquiring the ability to provide constructive feedback. For example, a woman might set a goal to actively listen without interruption during team

meetings or express her opinions confidently during brainstorming sessions.

Setting Boundaries:

Short-term goals in assertiveness often involve establishing and communicating personal boundaries. This entails recognizing one's limits and clearly communicating them to others. For instance, a woman may set a goal to say "no" when she feels overwhelmed with additional responsibilities, without feeling guilty or obliged to comply.

II. Long-term Goals: Empowering Women for Success

Career Advancement:

Long-term assertiveness goals can revolve around career progression and achieving professional success. This may involve setting goals such as seeking leadership roles, negotiating promotions, or advocating for equal opportunities in the workplace. For example, a woman may aspire to become a team leader within a specific timeframe or strive to close the gender pay gap in her organization.

Building Supportive Networks:
Establishing a strong support network is essential for long-term assertiveness goals. This can include surrounding oneself with like-minded individuals, mentors, or professional associations. A long-term goal could be to actively engage in networking events, join industry-specific communities, or seek out mentorship opportunities to gain insights and guidance from experienced professionals.

Empowering Other Women:
A significant aspect of assertiveness as a woman is uplifting and supporting other women. Long-term goals may involve initiatives to mentor, sponsor, or advocate for fellow women in various spheres of life. For instance, a woman may aim to establish a mentoring program within her organization or become involved in community initiatives that empower underrepresented women.

Defining short-term and long-term goals in assertiveness allows women to harness their inner strength, embrace their unique qualities, and navigate both personal and professional realms with confidence. By setting short-term goals that focus on self-awareness, communication skills, and boundaries, women can lay a strong foundation for assertiveness. Simultaneously, long-term goals centered around career advancement, building supportive networks, and empowering others pave the way for sustainable success. As women continue to embrace their assertive potential, they contribute to a more inclusive and equitable society, inspiring generations to come.

Breaking down goals into manageable steps

Setting goals is an essential part of personal and professional growth. However, sometimes goals can seem overwhelming or unattainable if they are not approached with a structured plan. We'll explore the significance of breaking down goals into manageable steps, enabling individuals to navigate their journey with clarity, focus, and a higher likelihood of success. We will discuss key strategies and provide examples that inspire You to take action and achieve their aspirations.

I. Understand the Power of Chunking: Dividing Goals into Smaller Tasks

Assess the Big Picture:
Before diving into goal breakdown, it is vital to have a clear understanding of the overarching objective. Take a moment to visualize the end result and ask yourself: What does success look like? This provides a solid foundation for breaking down the goal into manageable steps.

Identify Key Milestones:
Once you have a clear vision, identify the major milestones or significant checkpoints along the way. These milestones serve as important progress markers and allow you to track your advancement. For instance, if your goal is to run a marathon, key milestones could be completing a 5K race, a half marathon, and finally, the full marathon.

Break it Down:
Take each milestone and further divide it into smaller tasks or sub-goals. This process, known as chunking, helps to make the overall goal less overwhelming. For instance, if you aim to learn a new language, you could break it down into sub-goals such as learning basic vocabulary, practicing conversational skills, and mastering grammar rules.

II. Setting Realistic Timeframes and Prioritizing Tasks

Establish Timeframes:
Assigning realistic deadlines to each task or sub-goal is crucial for maintaining momentum and a sense of urgency. Consider the complexity and importance of each task, and allocate appropriate timeframes accordingly. This helps you stay on track and avoid procrastination. For example, if your goal is to write a book, you could set deadlines for completing each chapter or section.

Prioritize Tasks:

Evaluate the order of importance and dependencies among your tasks. Determine which tasks require completion before others can be initiated. By prioritizing tasks, you ensure a logical progression towards your goal. For instance, if you are launching a new business, tasks like market research and product development may take priority over designing a website.

III. Track Progress and Celebrate Achievements

Create a Progress Tracker:

Utilize a visual tool or a digital tracker to monitor your progress. This can be as simple as a checklist or a more detailed project management software. Regularly update and review your progress tracker to stay motivated and on top of your goals.

Celebrate Milestones:

Celebrating achievements, no matter how small, boosts motivation and reinforces positive habits. Take the time to acknowledge and reward yourself when you reach significant milestones or complete challenging tasks. This can be as simple as treating yourself to a favorite activity or sharing your accomplishment with friends and loved ones.

Breaking down goals into manageable steps is a transformative approach that empowers individuals to overcome overwhelm, maintain focus, and achieve success. By understanding the power of chunking, setting realistic timeframes, and prioritizing tasks, you can approach your goals with clarity and confidence. Remember to track your progress and celebrate achievements along the way. With a structured plan in place, you can unleash your potential, accomplish remarkable feats, and realize your dreams.

IV. Embrace Flexibility and Adaptability

Remain Flexible:

As you embark on your journey of pursuing your goals, it is essential to maintain a flexible mindset. Recognize that circumstances may change, unexpected obstacles may arise, and adjustments may be necessary. Embrace the ability to adapt your plan when needed while keeping your ultimate goal in sight.

Learn from Setbacks:
Setbacks are a natural part of any journey. Instead of viewing them as failures, see them as valuable learning opportunities. Analyze what went wrong, identify areas for improvement, and adjust your approach accordingly. By viewing setbacks as stepping stones rather than roadblocks, you can grow stronger and more resilient.

V. Seek Support and Accountability

Engage a Support System:
Surround yourself with a supportive network of individuals who believe in your goals and aspirations. Share your progress, challenges, and achievements with trusted friends, family members, or mentors who can offer guidance, encouragement, and valuable insights. Their support can help you stay motivated and navigate obstacles along the way.

Find an Accountability Partner:

Consider partnering with someone who shares similar goals or aspirations. An accountability partner can provide mutual support, hold each other responsible for progress, and provide constructive feedback. Regular check-ins and discussions can help you stay focused and committed to your journey.

VI.　Continual Evaluation and Refinement

Regularly Assess Your Progress:

Periodically evaluate your progress and assess if your current strategies and actions are aligning with your desired outcomes. Are there any adjustments or refinements that need to be made? Be open to reassessing and adapting your approach as necessary to ensure continued progress towards your goals.

Set New Milestones:

As you achieve your initial milestones, set new ones to keep the momentum going. Continually challenging yourself and setting new goals ensures ongoing growth and personal development. Embrace the mindset of lifelong learning and improvement.

Breaking down goals into manageable steps is a powerful strategy that empowers individuals to make progress, stay motivated, and achieve their aspirations. By embracing flexibility, seeking support, and continually evaluating and refining your approach, you set yourself up for long-term success. Remember, the journey towards your goals is just as important as reaching the destination. Embrace the process, celebrate your achievements, and enjoy the growth and transformation that comes from pursuing your dreams with a structured and strategic mindset.

Celebrating achievements and learning from setbacks

In the pursuit of personal and professional success, women encounter a variety of challenges and triumphs. It is essential to develop a mindset that celebrates achievements and learns from setbacks, as they provide valuable opportunities for growth and empowerment. We will delve into the importance of self-reflection, resilience, and the transformative power of these experiences. Let us uncover how celebrating achievements and learning from setbacks can propel women towards greater accomplishments.

I. Celebrating Achievements: Empowering Confidence and Motivation

Recognize Milestones:
Celebrating achievements begins with acknowledging and recognizing the milestones along your journey. Whether big or small, each accomplishment deserves recognition. Take the time to appreciate your efforts, hard work, and the progress you have made. By celebrating milestones, you cultivate a sense of accomplishment and boost your confidence.

Embrace Self-Reflection:
Reflecting on your achievements allows you to gain deeper insights into your strengths, growth, and areas of improvement. Consider what you have learned, the skills you have

developed, and the challenges you have overcome. This self-reflection fuels personal growth and equips you with the confidence to tackle new endeavors.

Share and Inspire:
Celebrating achievements is not only about personal gratification but also about inspiring and uplifting others. Share your successes with colleagues, friends, and mentors, providing them with a source of inspiration and motivation. By sharing your journey, you contribute to a culture of support and empowerment for women.

Example: If you successfully completed a challenging project at work, celebrate by sharing your achievements during team meetings, highlighting the lessons learned, and encouraging your colleagues to strive for excellence.

II. Learning from Setbacks: Building Resilience and Perseverance

Embrace the Growth Mindset:
Setbacks are not failures but opportunities for growth. Adopting a growth mindset allows you to view setbacks as valuable lessons and stepping stones toward success. Instead of being discouraged, see setbacks as an invitation to learn, adapt, and become stronger.

Analyze and Learn:
When facing setbacks, take the time to analyze what went wrong and why. Identify areas for improvement and consider alternative approaches or strategies. Learning from setbacks provides valuable insights that can inform future decisions and actions.

Cultivate Resilience:
Resilience is the ability to bounce back from adversity. By embracing setbacks as temporary hurdles, you develop resilience and the determination to persevere. Focus on your strengths, seek support, and maintain a positive mindset as you navigate challenges.

Example: If a business venture did not yield the expected results, reflect on the factors that led to the setback. Consider seeking guidance from mentors or industry experts, refining your strategy, and leveraging the lessons learned to embark on a new and improved endeavor.

III. Balancing Self-Compassion and Accountability

Practice Self-Compassion:
When facing setbacks, it is crucial to be kind to yourself. Treat setbacks as learning experiences rather than reasons for self-criticism. Acknowledge that setbacks are a natural part of the journey towards success. Embrace self-compassion and remind yourself of your resilience and capability.

Maintain Accountability:
While practicing self-compassion, it is equally important to hold yourself accountable. Take ownership of your actions, decisions, and their consequences. Use setbacks as opportunities to reflect on your approach and make necessary adjustments. Embrace accountability as a means to continually improve and grow.

Celebrating achievements and learning from setbacks are integral aspects of personal and professional growth for women.

Chapter 3

Effective Communication Skills

The role of communication in assertiveness as a woman

Assertiveness is a valuable skill that empowers individuals to express their thoughts, needs, and boundaries while respecting the rights of others. For women, assertiveness can be particularly significant, as societal expectations and gender norms often discourage them from being forthright and self-assured. However, effective communication lies at the heart of assertiveness, enabling women to navigate both personal and professional spheres with confidence and authenticity. We will explore the indispensable role of communication in fostering assertiveness among women, emphasizing its power to inspire positive change and cultivate personal growth.

Self-Awareness and Authentic Expression:

Communication serves as a vehicle for self-awareness, enabling women to identify and articulate their beliefs, desires, and emotions. By understanding themselves better, women can communicate their needs more assertively, expressing their thoughts and opinions with clarity, conviction, and authenticity. By fostering self-awareness, communication empowers women to set boundaries, make informed decisions, and advocate for themselves effectively.

Overcoming Gender Stereotypes and Cultural Barriers:

In many cultures, women are expected to conform to certain gender stereotypes, which often discourage assertiveness. Effective communication can help challenge these societal expectations by providing women with the tools to convey their ideas confidently, regardless of preconceived notions. By developing strong communication skills, women can counteract biases, dismantle stereotypes, and break through barriers that may hinder their assertiveness.

Active Listening and Empathy:
Communication is a two-way process that involves not only expressing oneself but also listening actively and empathetically. Women who actively listen and show empathy create an environment that fosters open dialogue and understanding. By understanding the perspectives and needs of others, women can engage in assertive communication that respects differing viewpoints, leading to more meaningful connections and constructive outcomes.

Negotiation and Conflict Resolution:
Assertiveness is not synonymous with aggression. Effective communication equips women with negotiation and conflict resolution skills, allowing them to assert their needs while maintaining positive relationships. By communicating assertively, women can navigate difficult conversations with confidence, address conflicts constructively, and find mutually beneficial solutions that

uphold their rights and desires without disregarding the needs of others.

Building Professional Success:
Communication plays a vital role in professional success, particularly for women aspiring to leadership positions. Effective communication skills, such as public speaking, persuasive writing, and assertive expression, are essential in establishing credibility, gaining influence, and inspiring others. By honing their communication abilities, women can break through glass ceilings, challenge gender disparities, and make their voices heard in the workplace.

The role of communication in fostering assertiveness among women cannot be overstated. It serves as the foundation upon which women can build their self-confidence, challenge societal expectations, and advocate for their rights and aspirations. By developing effective communication skills, women can express themselves authentically, overcome gender stereotypes, navigate conflicts, and achieve success in both personal and professional realms. Embracing assertive communication empowers women to forge their own paths, make meaningful contributions, and inspire positive change in their lives and communities.

The role of communication in assertiveness in assertiveness

Assertiveness is a crucial attribute that empowers individuals to express their thoughts, needs, and boundaries effectively while maintaining respect for others. For women, assertiveness holds particular significance, as societal expectations and gender norms often discourage them from being self-assured and outspoken. However, the key to developing assertiveness lies in mastering effective communication skills. We delve into the vital role that communication plays in cultivating assertiveness among women, emphasizing its power to inspire personal growth and professional success.

Self-Reflection and Self-Expression:
Communication serves as a powerful tool for self-reflection, enabling women to gain a deeper understanding of their beliefs, desires, and emotions. By enhancing self-awareness, effective communication facilitates the expression of thoughts and opinions with clarity, confidence, and authenticity. Through skillful communication, women can effectively communicate their needs, establish boundaries, and assert their viewpoints, empowering themselves in the process.

Overcoming Societal Expectations and Stereotypes:
Women often face societal pressures to conform to specific gender roles and stereotypes, which can hinder assertiveness. By developing strong communication skills, women can challenge these expectations and stereotypes. Effective communication empowers women to express their ideas and thoughts confidently, regardless of preconceived notions, and assert their rights and opinions with conviction. By breaking free from societal constraints, women can cultivate

assertiveness and pave the way for positive change.

Active Listening and Empathy:

Communication is a two-way process that encompasses not only expressing oneself but also actively listening and showing empathy towards others. By honing active listening skills, women can create an environment that fosters open dialogue and understanding. Empathy plays a crucial role in assertiveness, allowing women to comprehend different perspectives and needs. By actively listening and empathizing, women can engage in assertive communication that respects diverse viewpoints, fostering meaningful connections and promoting constructive outcomes.

Effective Negotiation and Conflict Resolution:

Assertiveness should never be equated with aggression. Effective communication equips women with negotiation and conflict resolution skills, enabling them to assert their needs while preserving positive relationships. By communicating assertively, women can navigate challenging conversations with confidence, address conflicts constructively, and seek mutually beneficial solutions that uphold their rights and desires while considering the needs of others. Through assertive communication, women can build bridges and resolve conflicts effectively.

Advancing Professional Growth:
Communication plays a pivotal role in professional success, especially for women aspiring to leadership roles. Proficient communication skills, including public speaking, persuasive writing, and assertive expression, are instrumental in establishing credibility, influencing others, and driving change. By honing their communication abilities, women can shatter glass ceilings, challenge gender disparities, and make their voices heard in the workplace. Assertive communication empowers women to navigate professional challenges, promote their ideas, and contribute meaningfully to their fields.

In the pursuit of assertiveness, effective communication stands as an indispensable pillar for women. By mastering communication skills, women can develop self-confidence, defy societal expectations, and advocate for their rights and aspirations. Through assertive communication, women can forge their paths, inspire positive change, and make significant contributions in their personal and professional lives. Communication acts as the catalyst for empowering women to embrace assertiveness, creating a world where their voices are heard, respected, and valued.

Developing active listening skills in assertiveness

Assertiveness is a powerful trait that allows individuals, particularly women, to confidently express their thoughts, needs, and boundaries. While assertiveness involves effective self-expression, it is equally essential to develop active listening skills as a crucial component of assertive communication. Active listening enables women to understand others' perspectives, build empathy, and engage in constructive dialogue. We explore the significance of developing active listening skills in fostering assertiveness among women.

Creating Meaningful Connections:
Active listening forms the foundation for meaningful connections and effective communication. By actively listening, women can demonstrate genuine interest in what others have to say, fostering a sense of respect and understanding. This empathetic approach encourages open dialogue, strengthens relationships, and creates an environment conducive to assertive communication. Through active listening, women can build rapport, foster trust, and establish mutually beneficial connections.

Enhancing Empathy and Understanding:
Active listening goes beyond merely hearing words; it involves a deep level of empathy and understanding. By actively engaging in conversations and paying attention to non-verbal cues, women can better comprehend others' emotions, concerns, and needs. Developing empathy through active

listening allows women to see situations from different perspectives, enhancing their ability to respond assertively with compassion and consideration.

Validating and Acknowledging Others:

One crucial aspect of assertive communication is acknowledging and validating others' experiences and viewpoints. Active listening enables women to express genuine interest and respect for what others have to say, even if they disagree. By actively acknowledging and validating others' perspectives, women can create an inclusive and supportive atmosphere, encouraging open discussions and collaborative problem-solving.

Overcoming Assumptions and Stereotypes:

Active listening helps women challenge assumptions and stereotypes that may hinder assertiveness. By actively listening without preconceived notions, women can overcome biases and judgments, allowing for a more accurate understanding of others' experiences. This approach fosters assertiveness by providing a solid foundation for effective communication based on respect and authenticity, regardless of societal expectations or stereotypes.

Constructive Conflict Resolution:

Active listening plays a pivotal role in assertive conflict resolution. When faced with conflicts, women can utilize active listening to understand the underlying issues, concerns, and emotions of all parties involved. By actively listening and demonstrating empathy, women can defuse tensions, seek common ground, and work towards mutually agreeable solutions. Active listening ensures that assertive communication during conflicts is focused on understanding, respect, and finding resolutions that uphold the rights and needs of everyone involved.

Developing active listening skills is a powerful tool for empowering assertiveness in women. By actively listening, women can establish meaningful connections, enhance empathy, and foster constructive dialogue. Active listening enables women to overcome assumptions and stereotypes, validating and acknowledging others' experiences while promoting inclusivity and respect. Moreover, active listening plays a crucial role in conflict resolution, ensuring assertive communication that seeks understanding and mutually beneficial solutions. By embracing active listening, women can amplify their assertiveness, create positive change, and forge stronger connections in both personal and professional spheres.

3.1 Clear and Direct Expression:

Communicating thoughts, needs, and boundaries effectively.

Assertiveness empowers women to express their thoughts, needs, and boundaries confidently while maintaining respect for themselves and others. Effective communication plays a pivotal role in developing assertiveness, enabling women to navigate diverse situations with clarity, authenticity, and self-assurance.

Expressing Thoughts with Clarity:

Assertive communication allows women to express their thoughts clearly and directly. Instead of tiptoeing around important issues, assertive women articulate their ideas without hesitation, using concise and assertive language. For example, in a team meeting, a woman confidently shares her innovative solution to a problem, clearly explaining the rationale behind it. By expressing thoughts with clarity, women establish themselves as confident contributors, promoting their ideas and gaining the respect of others.

Asserting Needs with Confidence:

Assertive communication empowers women to assert their needs confidently, ensuring they are heard and respected. For instance, in a professional setting, a woman requests a well-deserved promotion by presenting her achievements and highlighting her contributions to the organization. By assertively expressing her need for career advancement, she establishes her value and demonstrates her commitment to personal growth. Effectively communicating needs enables women to advocate for themselves, fostering assertiveness in various aspects of life.

Establishing Firm Boundaries:

Assertiveness equips women with the ability to establish and maintain firm boundaries. Women who effectively communicate their boundaries create a sense of self-respect and ensure that their limits are respected by others. In a personal relationship, a woman openly communicates her need for personal space and privacy, asserting her boundaries firmly yet respectfully. By doing so, she cultivates a healthier dynamic that encourages mutual respect and self-care, contributing to her overall well-being and assertiveness.

Overcoming Fear of Rejection or Conflict:

Assertive communication helps women overcome the fear of rejection or conflict that often hinders effective self-expression. By embracing assertiveness, women learn to communicate their thoughts, needs, and boundaries even in challenging situations. For example, a woman confidently declines an invitation to participate in a project that does not align with her interests or workload capacity, clearly explaining her reasons while maintaining a positive rapport. By overcoming the fear of conflict and rejection, women assert their autonomy and cultivate healthy assertive relationships.

Seeking Constructive Resolutions:
Assertive communication fosters a problem-solving approach, allowing women to seek constructive resolutions when conflicts or disagreements arise. For instance, in a team setting, a woman addresses a disagreement by actively listening to others' perspectives, expressing her concerns assertively, and collaborating on finding a solution that meets everyone's needs. By engaging in assertive communication, she promotes open dialogue, mutual understanding, and a harmonious work environment.

Communicating thoughts, needs, and boundaries effectively is a crucial component of assertiveness for women. Through assertive communication, women express their thoughts with clarity, assert their needs with confidence, and establish firm boundaries. By overcoming the fear of rejection or conflict, women can advocate for themselves and seek constructive resolutions, fostering healthy relationships and personal growth. Real instances demonstrate the transformative power of assertive communication, showcasing how women can assert their voices, promote their ideas, and navigate various aspects of life with authenticity and self-assurance. By embracing effective communication, women can unlock their assertiveness and inspire positive change in themselves and their communities.

Using "I" statements to express opinions and preferences.

Assertiveness is a powerful attribute that enables individuals, especially women, to express their opinions and preferences confidently while maintaining respect for themselves and others. One effective communication technique in assertiveness is using "I" statements. These statements allow women to assert their thoughts and desires without sounding confrontational or dismissive.

Personal Ownership of Thoughts and Feelings:

Using "I" statements emphasizes personal ownership and responsibility for one's thoughts and feelings. By beginning a statement with "I," women communicate that they are expressing their own perspective and emotions, rather than making assumptions or judgments about others. For example, instead of saying, "You always interrupt me," an assertive woman might say, "I feel frustrated when I am interrupted." This approach encourages open dialogue and invites respectful engagement.

Promoting Effective Communication:

"I" statements promote effective communication by focusing on individual experiences rather than attributing blame or making generalizations. When women use "I" statements to express their opinions and preferences, they create an environment that encourages understanding and collaboration. For instance, instead of saying, "You never listen to me," an assertive woman might say, "I would appreciate it if you could listen attentively when I am speaking." This approach fosters constructive dialogue and increases the likelihood of being heard and understood.

Encouraging Respectful Assertiveness:
Using "I" statements allows women to assert their opinions and preferences assertively while maintaining respect for others. By framing statements in terms of personal experience, women avoid coming across as aggressive or confrontational. For instance, instead of saying, "You're wrong," an assertive woman might say, "I have a different perspective on this matter." This approach creates space for diverse viewpoints and encourages respectful exchange of ideas.

Enhancing Active Listening and Empathy:
"I" statements promote active listening and empathy in assertive communication. When women use these statements, they encourage others to genuinely listen and consider their perspective. By expressing thoughts and

preferences in a non-threatening manner, women create an opportunity for empathy and understanding. For example, saying, "I feel overwhelmed when there is excessive noise in the office" invites others to acknowledge and empathize with the woman's experience, fostering a more supportive and conducive environment.

Strengthening Relationships and Collaboration:

Using "I" statements fosters stronger relationships and promotes collaboration. By expressing opinions and preferences assertively, women assert their needs while maintaining open lines of communication. This approach encourages others to reciprocate with their own perspectives, enabling the development of more inclusive and collaborative solutions. By using "I" statements, women create a foundation for constructive dialogue and cooperative relationships.

Using "I" statements is a powerful tool in expressing opinions and preferences assertively as a woman. By emphasizing personal ownership, promoting effective communication, and encouraging respectful assertiveness, "I" statements allow women to assert their thoughts and desires while maintaining respect for themselves and others. Furthermore, this communication technique enhances active listening, empathy, and collaboration, strengthening relationships and promoting a culture of open dialogue. By embracing the power of "I" statements, women can unlock their assertiveness, inspire positive change, and foster meaningful connections in both personal and professional realms.

Constructive confrontation and conflict resolution techniques.

Assertiveness empowers women to express themselves confidently, but it also encompasses the ability to confront conflicts and resolve them constructively. Constructive confrontation and conflict resolution techniques play a vital role in assertiveness, enabling women to navigate difficult conversations with grace, respect, and effectiveness. We will see the significance of these techniques in fostering assertiveness as a woman, providing practical guidance on how to employ them for successful conflict resolution.

Maintaining Calm and Composure:

In constructive confrontation and conflict resolution, maintaining a calm and composed demeanor is essential. As a woman, staying composed allows you to assert your thoughts and needs confidently, without succumbing to emotional reactions. By remaining calm, you establish a positive environment for effective communication, enabling a more productive resolution of conflicts.

Active Listening and Empathy:

Active listening and empathy are foundational skills in conflict resolution. By actively listening, women can understand the perspectives and concerns of all parties involved, fostering empathy and establishing a foundation for constructive dialogue. Through empathy, you demonstrate understanding and validate the feelings and experiences of others, fostering an atmosphere of respect and openness.

Clarifying Intentions and Interests:
Constructive confrontation involves clarifying intentions and interests. Clearly expressing your intentions and desired outcomes helps others understand your perspective and motivations. It is equally important to seek clarity on the intentions and interests of the other party. By actively exploring and understanding each other's underlying needs, you can identify common ground and work toward mutually beneficial solutions.

Using Non-Violent Communication:
Non-violent communication techniques are valuable tools in assertive conflict resolution. Employing "I" statements, expressing feelings and needs, and avoiding blame or judgment help to create a non-confrontational atmosphere. For example, instead of saying, "You never listen to me," you can use an "I" statement: "I feel unheard when my opinions are interrupted." This approach encourages

open dialogue and minimizes defensiveness, promoting a more constructive resolution.

Collaborative Problem-Solving:

A key aspect of assertive conflict resolution is adopting a collaborative problem-solving approach. Instead of viewing conflict as a win-lose situation, seek win-win solutions that address the needs of all parties involved. Encourage brainstorming and creative thinking to explore alternative solutions and find common ground. By working together, women can foster understanding, build stronger relationships, and reach mutually satisfactory resolutions.

Seeking Mediation or Facilitation:

In complex or deeply entrenched conflicts, seeking mediation or facilitation can be beneficial. A neutral third party can help guide the conversation, ensure equal participation, and maintain a focus on constructive dialogue. Mediation provides an opportunity to resolve conflicts more effectively, promoting assertiveness and preserving relationships.

Embracing Continuous Learning:
Assertive conflict resolution requires ongoing learning and growth. Reflect on past experiences and seek opportunities to improve your conflict resolution skills. By continuously learning and refining your approach, you enhance your assertiveness and become better equipped to navigate conflicts successfully.

Constructive confrontation and conflict resolution techniques are integral to assertiveness as a woman. By maintaining composure, practicing active listening and empathy, and employing non-violent communication, women can navigate conflicts effectively and assert their needs with respect. Embracing collaborative problem-solving and seeking mediation when necessary enhances the resolution process, fostering stronger relationships and empowering assertiveness. By embracing continuous learning and growth, women can cultivate their conflict resolution skills, inspiring positive change in themselves and the world around them.

3.2 Active Listening and Empathy:

Developing attentive listening skills.

In today's fast-paced world, effective communication has become more critical than ever. As a woman seeking to enhance your assertiveness, mastering the art of attentive listening can empower you to express your thoughts, needs, and desires with confidence. Cultivating this essential skill not only strengthens your assertiveness but also fosters deeper connections, enriches relationships, and encourages mutual understanding.

Understanding the Importance of Attentive Listening:
Attentive listening involves more than just hearing the words spoken by others. It encompasses a mindful and empathetic approach, where you fully engage with the speaker, absorb their message, and convey genuine interest. By actively practicing attentive listening, you demonstrate respect, validate others' perspectives, and build trust,

establishing a solid foundation for assertive communication.

Enhancing Self-Awareness:

Before embarking on your journey to becoming an attentive listener, it's essential to cultivate self-awareness. Reflect on your communication style, identifying any patterns or tendencies that hinder effective listening. Acknowledge any preconceived notions or biases that may influence your ability to truly hear others. Developing self-awareness allows you to approach conversations with openness and a willingness to learn from different viewpoints.

Practicing Mindfulness:

Mindfulness serves as a powerful tool in developing attentive listening skills. It involves focusing your attention on the present moment, suspending judgment, and fully immersing yourself in the conversation at hand. Avoid distractions, such as multitasking or preoccupying thoughts, and direct your energy towards actively understanding the speaker's words, body language, and emotions. By mindfully engaging in the dialogue, you create an atmosphere of respect and attentiveness.

Non-Verbal Communication:
Listening is not limited to hearing words alone. Non-verbal cues play a significant role in effective communication. Pay attention to the speaker's facial expressions, body language, and tone of voice. These subtle signals often convey underlying emotions and provide valuable insights into the speaker's message. By being attuned to non-verbal cues, you demonstrate empathy and understanding, enhancing your ability to respond assertively and appropriately.

Empathy and Validation:
Empathy forms the cornerstone of attentive listening. By putting yourself in the speaker's shoes and trying to understand their perspective, you foster a deeper connection. Show genuine interest and validate their feelings, experiences, and concerns. Empathetic listening allows you to respond thoughtfully and constructively, building trust and nurturing assertive communication.

Active Engagement:

Active engagement is a key component of attentive listening. Through active engagement, you demonstrate your involvement in the conversation and encourage the speaker to express themselves fully. Utilize verbal cues such as nodding, summarizing their points, and asking clarifying questions. Engaging actively not only helps you comprehend the message better but also reassures the speaker that you value their input, promoting assertiveness in both parties.

Reflective Listening:

Practice reflective listening to solidify your understanding and demonstrate your attentiveness. After the speaker shares their thoughts, paraphrase their main points and reflect them back to ensure accuracy. This not only shows that you were actively listening but also gives the speaker an opportunity to clarify any misunderstandings. Reflective listening validates their message and encourages open and assertive communication.

Avoiding Interrupting and Judging:
Interrupting or jumping to conclusions while someone is speaking can hinder attentive listening and assertive communication. Give the speaker ample space to express their thoughts without interruption, and resist the urge to interject with your own opinions or judgments. By patiently allowing them to finish their point, you create a supportive environment that encourages assertiveness and fosters effective dialogue.

Seeking Clarification:
In the pursuit of attentive listening, it is crucial to seek clarification when needed. If you encounter unfamiliar terms, ambiguous statements, or conflicting information, politely ask for further explanation or examples. Seeking clarification demonstrates your commitment to understanding the speaker's perspective accurately, and it contributes to building a foundation of trust and mutual respect.

Continuous Learning and Improvement: Developing attentive listening skills is an ongoing process that requires dedication and practice. Embrace every opportunity to refine your skills by actively seeking feedback from trusted individuals. Engage in workshops, seminars, or online resources that focus on effective communication and assertiveness. By continuously learning and improving, you position yourself as a confident and attentive listener, capable of expressing your thoughts assertively.

As a woman seeking to enhance assertiveness, attentive listening is an invaluable skill that can propel your communication to new heights. By cultivating self-awareness, practicing mindfulness, and engaging actively, you lay the groundwork for meaningful connections and assertive expression. Remember, attentive listening is a continuous journey of learning and improvement. Embrace the power of listening and watch as your assertiveness flourishes, empowering you to confidently communicate your needs, desires, and ideas while fostering harmonious relationships.

Encouraging open and honest communication in others

Open and honest communication is a cornerstone of assertiveness, enabling individuals to express themselves authentically and build strong, meaningful connections. As a woman seeking to foster assertiveness in yourself and those around you, encouraging open and honest communication is a powerful tool. By creating a safe and supportive environment, you can empower others to share their thoughts, feelings, and ideas confidently.

Creating a Safe and Judgment-Free Space:

To encourage open and honest communication, it is vital to establish a safe and judgment-free space. Ensure that individuals feel comfortable expressing themselves without fear of criticism or ridicule. Foster an environment of respect, actively listening to others' perspectives and valuing their contributions. By setting the tone for inclusivity and understanding, you inspire others to share their thoughts and opinions openly.

Active and Attentive Listening:

Active and attentive listening is a catalyst for open and honest communication. Give your undivided attention to the speaker, maintaining eye contact, and using non-verbal cues to show interest and engagement. Encourage individuals to express themselves fully by asking open-ended questions and seeking clarification when needed. By practicing active listening, you convey respect and validate the speaker's experiences, nurturing an atmosphere conducive to assertive expression.

Embracing Empathy and Understanding:

Empathy and understanding are powerful tools for encouraging open and honest communication. Put yourself in others' shoes, seeking to understand their perspectives and emotions. Show genuine empathy by acknowledging their feelings and experiences. Create a supportive environment where individuals feel heard, accepted, and validated.

By cultivating empathy and understanding, you empower others to share their thoughts and concerns openly, fostering assertiveness and strengthening interpersonal connections.

Constructive Feedback and Appreciation:

Offering constructive feedback and appreciation encourages open communication by creating a culture of growth and recognition. When providing feedback, focus on specific behaviors or actions rather than personal attacks. Be constructive, highlighting areas for improvement while offering suggestions and support. Similarly, acknowledge and appreciate individuals' contributions, reinforcing their confidence and motivation to communicate openly. By balancing feedback and appreciation, you foster an environment where open dialogue thrives.

Encouraging Diverse Perspectives:

Promote the value of diverse perspectives and encourage individuals to express their unique viewpoints. Emphasize the importance of inclusivity, recognizing that different backgrounds and experiences enrich conversations and decision-making processes. Actively seek out diverse opinions and create opportunities for everyone to contribute. By embracing diverse perspectives, you foster a culture of open-mindedness, where assertiveness flourishes, and innovative ideas emerge.

Active Conflict Resolution:

Conflict is an inevitable part of communication, but it can be an opportunity for growth and deeper understanding. Encourage open and honest communication during conflicts by promoting active and respectful dialogue. Create a space where individuals can express their concerns, listen to one another, and find mutually beneficial solutions. Encourage assertive communication techniques, such as using "I" statements and focusing on the issue at hand, to ensure conflicts are addressed constructively.

Leading by Example:

As a woman striving to encourage open and honest communication, it is essential to lead by example. Practice what you preach by being open, honest, and assertive in your own communication. Share your thoughts, concerns, and ideas openly, demonstrating vulnerability and authenticity. By modeling assertiveness and open communication, you inspire others to follow suit, creating a positive ripple effect within your personal and professional circles.

Chapter 4

Assertiveness in Various Settings

Applying assertiveness skills in different aspects of life.

By mastering assertiveness, women can navigate various aspects of life with grace, authenticity, and self-assurance. We will learn the importance of assertiveness skills and provide practical insights on applying them in different domains of life, from personal relationships to professional settings.

Assertiveness in Personal Relationships: In personal relationships, assertiveness plays a vital role in establishing healthy boundaries, fostering open communication, and maintaining mutual respect. Women who cultivate assertiveness skills can confidently express their emotions, opinions, and desires, leading to deeper connections and increased satisfaction. By setting clear boundaries and expressing personal needs assertively, women can navigate conflicts effectively and build strong, fulfilling relationships.

Assertiveness in the Workplace:

Assertiveness is a valuable asset for women in the professional realm, where self-advocacy and effective communication are essential. By asserting their ideas, opinions, and ambitions, women can assert their presence and contribute meaningfully to their organizations. Assertiveness helps women negotiate fair compensation, secure career advancements, and overcome gender biases. By practicing assertiveness, women can confidently voice their opinions, take on leadership roles, and create positive change within their workplaces.

Assertiveness in Academic Settings:

In academic environments, assertiveness is key to success. By actively participating in class discussions, asking questions, and seeking clarification, women can deepen their understanding and demonstrate their engagement. Assertive communication with professors and peers can lead to meaningful collaborations, networking opportunities, and academic growth. By advocating for themselves, women can ensure equal opportunities for their education and advancement.

Assertiveness in Social Situations:

Assertiveness is equally important in social situations, where women often face societal expectations and pressure. By asserting their preferences, women can choose activities that align with their interests and values, instead of conforming to others' expectations. Assertiveness helps women set limits on their time, energy, and commitments, ensuring they prioritize self-care and pursue activities that bring them joy and fulfillment.

Assertiveness in Health and Wellness:

Assertiveness plays a crucial role in maintaining physical and mental well-being. Women who are assertive can prioritize self-care, set boundaries around their time and energy, and advocate for their healthcare needs. Assertiveness empowers women to communicate effectively with healthcare professionals, ask questions, and make informed decisions about their bodies and overall health.

Assertiveness is a powerful skill that empowers women in every aspect of life. By cultivating assertiveness, women can confidently express their needs, desires, and boundaries, leading to more fulfilling personal relationships, successful careers, academic achievements, and overall well-being. By embracing assertiveness, women can break free from societal expectations, challenge gender biases, and create positive change in their lives and the world around them. Embrace assertiveness and unlock your true potential as a woman of strength and influence.

Recognizing the unique challenges women may face in different settings

Women face a range of unique challenges in various settings, from personal to professional, due to societal norms, gender biases, and cultural expectations. Recognizing and understanding these challenges is crucial for fostering empathy, promoting equality, and empowering women.

Personal Relationships:

In personal relationships, women often face expectations regarding traditional gender roles and societal norms. They may encounter challenges related to unequal distribution of household chores, emotional labor, and unrealistic beauty standards. Recognizing and addressing these challenges is vital for promoting healthier, more equitable relationships where both partners share responsibilities and support each other's personal growth and well-being.

Professional Settings:

Women encounter a myriad of challenges in the workplace, including gender bias, limited opportunities for advancement, and wage disparities. Recognizing the unique barriers women face in professional settings is essential for creating inclusive work environments. By challenging gender stereotypes, implementing equitable policies, and fostering mentorship and sponsorship programs, organizations can create opportunities for women to thrive, excel, and break through the glass ceiling.

Academic Settings:

Despite progress, women still face unique challenges in academic settings. Gender biases can affect educational opportunities, discourage participation in certain fields, and hinder career advancement. Recognizing and addressing these challenges requires promoting gender equality in educational institutions, encouraging female representation in STEM and other traditionally male-dominated fields, and providing support systems to help women navigate the academic landscape with confidence and success.

Entrepreneurship:

Women who embark on entrepreneurial ventures often encounter gender-specific challenges. Access to funding, networking opportunities, and mentorship are areas where women face significant disparities. Recognizing and rectifying these challenges involves promoting inclusive entrepreneurship ecosystems, providing training and financial support tailored to women's needs, and fostering networks that empower women to navigate the entrepreneurial landscape successfully.

Health and Wellness:
Women face unique challenges in maintaining their physical and mental well-being. Issues such as reproductive health, body image, and gender-specific diseases require specialized attention and support. Recognizing these challenges involves creating safe spaces for discussions, promoting comprehensive healthcare services that address women's specific needs, and challenging societal expectations that impact women's self-perception and self-care practices.

Recognizing the unique challenges women face in different settings is a crucial step towards promoting gender equality and empowerment. By acknowledging and understanding these hurdles, we can work collectively to break down barriers, challenge biases, and create inclusive environments that allow women to thrive. Through education, advocacy, and policy changes, we can ensure that women receive equal opportunities, respect, and support in personal relationships, professional settings, academia, entrepreneurship, and health and wellness domains. Together, let us strive for a world where women can navigate every setting with confidence, authenticity, and success.

Strategies for adapting assertiveness to specific situations

Developing assertiveness skills is essential for women to effectively communicate their needs, express their opinions, and establish boundaries. However, it is equally important to recognize that assertiveness may require adaptability in different situations. This presents strategies to help women adapt their assertiveness approach to specific contexts, empowering them to navigate diverse scenarios with confidence and clarity.

Assertiveness in Personal Relationships: Case: Sarah, a woman in a romantic relationship, wants to express her dissatisfaction with her partner's behavior without causing unnecessary conflict.

Strategy: Use "I" Statements and Active Listening

In this situation, Sarah can employ the use of "I" statements to express her feelings without blaming her partner. By saying, "I feel hurt when..." instead of "You always make me feel..." she takes ownership of her emotions and encourages open dialogue. Additionally, active listening plays a crucial role in understanding her partner's perspective, promoting mutual respect, and fostering effective communication.

Assertiveness in Professional Settings:

Case: Emma, a woman in a male-dominated workplace, wants to assert her ideas during team meetings without being overshadowed.

Strategy: Prepare and Practice Assertive Communication

To adapt assertiveness in professional settings, Emma can prepare her thoughts and ideas in advance, ensuring she is well-informed and confident when expressing herself. It is crucial to practice assertive communication techniques, such as maintaining eye contact, speaking clearly, and using confident body language. Emma can also engage in assertive behaviors, such as respectfully interrupting when necessary, to ensure her ideas receive the attention they deserve.

Assertiveness in Negotiations:

Case: Lisa, a woman negotiating a salary increase, wants to advocate for fair compensation without coming across as overly aggressive.

Strategy: Present Objective Data and Highlight Value

To adapt assertiveness in negotiations, Lisa can gather objective data on industry standards and salary ranges to support her request for fair compensation. By focusing on the value she brings to the organization, emphasizing her achievements and contributions, Lisa can demonstrate her worth and strengthen her negotiating position. Additionally, maintaining a calm and composed demeanor throughout the negotiation process will project confidence and professionalism.

Assertiveness in Social Settings:

Case: Rachel, a woman attending a social gathering, wants to assert her boundaries and decline unwanted advances politely.

Strategy: Use Assertive Language and Non-Verbal Cues

Rachel can use assertive language to clearly communicate her boundaries, such as saying, "No, thank you. I'm not interested" or "I appreciate the offer, but I'm not comfortable with that." She can support her words with assertive body language, including maintaining a confident posture, making direct eye contact, and using appropriate gestures. These strategies help Rachel maintain her autonomy and assert her boundaries while preserving social harmony.

Assertiveness in Parenting:

Case: Jessica, a mother, wants to establish clear expectations and rules for her children without resorting to aggression or authoritarianism.

Strategy: Use Positive Reinforcement and Active Listening

Jessica can adapt assertiveness in parenting by using positive reinforcement to encourage desired behavior in her children. By praising and acknowledging their efforts, Jessica creates a supportive environment that fosters open communication. Additionally, active listening allows Jessica to understand her children's perspectives and concerns, fostering a sense of respect and cooperation within the parent-child relationship.

Adapting assertiveness to specific situations empowers women to navigate various contexts effectively. By employing strategies tailored to personal relationships, professional settings, negotiations, social situations, and parenting, women can assert their needs, express their opinions, and establish boundaries with confidence and clarity. Remember, adaptability is key, and by practicing these strategies, women can harness the power of assertiveness in diverse scenarios, creating positive change

4.1 Assertiveness at Work:

Navigating Power Dynamics and Overcoming Gender Bias

Assertiveness is a vital skill for women, allowing them to express themselves confidently and effectively. However, navigating power dynamics and overcoming gender bias can present unique challenges. This strategies will help women to navigate these obstacles and embrace assertiveness in the face of gender-based biases and power imbalances.

Recognizing Power Dynamics:

Case: Emily, a woman in a position of lower authority, needs to assert herself with a male colleague in a higher position without undermining their working relationship.

Strategy: Build Credibility and Confidence

Emily can navigate power dynamics by building her credibility through thorough preparation, being knowledgeable about the subject matter, and presenting her ideas with confidence. By emphasizing her expertise, she can assert herself while maintaining a respectful tone. It is crucial for Emily to leverage her strengths and demonstrate her value, ensuring her ideas are given due consideration.

Overcoming Gender Bias:
Case: Maria, a woman facing gender bias in a predominantly male work environment, wants to assert herself without being dismissed or undermined due to her gender.
Strategy: Own Your Achievements and Use Assertive Communication

Maria can overcome gender bias by actively owning her achievements and confidently asserting her opinions. By focusing on facts, data, and evidence to support her ideas, Maria can challenge any bias and demonstrate her competence. Using assertive communication techniques, such as speaking with clarity, maintaining eye contact, and using assertive body language, Maria can command respect and ensure her contributions are recognized and valued.

Establishing Boundaries:

Case: Sarah, a woman struggling with boundary violations, wants to assert herself firmly while maintaining professionalism in her workplace.

Strategy: Assertive Statements and Non-Negotiable Boundaries

Sarah can establish and communicate her boundaries clearly and assertively. By using "I" statements, she can express her discomfort and expectations directly, such as saying, "I feel uncomfortable when my personal space is invaded, and I expect it to be respected." Sarah can reinforce her boundaries with firm yet professional language, leaving no room for negotiation. It is crucial for Sarah to maintain consistency and reinforce her boundaries when they are crossed.

Overcoming Interruptions:

Case: Jessica, a woman frequently interrupted during meetings, wants to assert herself and ensure her ideas are heard and valued.

Strategy: Interruption Awareness and Assertive Interruption Handling

Jessica can raise awareness about interruptions by gently addressing them when they occur. She can say, "Excuse me, I was not finished speaking," or redirect the conversation back to her original point. By maintaining a confident and assertive tone, Jessica can establish her presence in meetings and ensure her ideas receive the attention they deserve. It is important for Jessica to be persistent and consistently assert herself against interruptions.

Building Allies and Support Networks:
Case: Rachel, a woman facing gender bias, wants to navigate assertiveness challenges by building alliances with like-minded individuals. Strategy: Seek Support and Collaborate

Rachel can find support by seeking out allies who share her experiences or who value gender equality. By forming strong connections and collaborating with others, Rachel can gain support, exchange strategies, and amplify her voice. Together, they can challenge biases, address gender inequalities, and create a more inclusive and supportive environment.

Navigating power dynamics and overcoming gender bias in assertiveness can be challenging for women. By recognizing power imbalances, overcoming bias, establishing boundaries, handling interruptions assertively, and building allies, women can navigate these obstacles and embrace assertiveness confidently. By empowering themselves and advocating for change, women can break through barriers, challenge gender biases, and create a more inclusive and equal playing field for assertiveness in all aspects of life. Remember, assertiveness is a powerful tool for

Negotiating salary, promotions, and opportunities

Negotiating salary, promotions, and opportunities is a crucial aspect of career advancement, and assertiveness plays a vital role in empowering women to advocate for their worth and achieve their professional goals. We will explore strategies and case studies that highlight how assertiveness can help women navigate the complexities of negotiating for fair compensation, promotions, and meaningful opportunities.

Negotiating Salary:

Case Study: Sarah, a highly skilled professional, wants to negotiate a competitive salary during a job offer to ensure fair compensation.
Strategy: Research, Preparation, and Effective Communication

Sarah can begin by conducting thorough research on industry salary ranges, job market conditions, and the specific value she brings to the organization. Armed with this knowledge, she can confidently articulate her expectations during the negotiation process. By using assertive communication techniques, such as clearly stating her desired salary, providing evidence of her qualifications, and emphasizing her value proposition, Sarah can negotiate a salary that reflects her worth and expertise.

Seeking Promotions:

Case Study: Emily, a woman who has consistently demonstrated exceptional performance, wants to assertively pursue a promotion within her organization.

Strategy: Self-Advocacy, Documented Achievements, and Building Relationships

Emily can assertively pursue a promotion by advocating for herself and actively communicating her aspirations to her supervisors. She can compile a comprehensive list of her achievements, showcasing tangible contributions, positive outcomes, and areas where she has gone above and beyond her current role. By building positive relationships with decision-makers, seeking mentorship, and actively participating in professional development opportunities, Emily can position herself as a strong candidate for promotion and assert her readiness for the next level.

Creating Opportunities:

Case Study: Maria, a woman with innovative ideas, wants to assertively create new opportunities within her organization to make a meaningful impact.

Strategy: Pitching Ideas, Networking, and Initiative

Maria can assertively create opportunities by pitching her innovative ideas to relevant stakeholders within her organization. By highlighting the potential benefits and addressing potential challenges, she can demonstrate her proactive mindset and problem-solving abilities. Maria can also leverage her network, actively seeking connections with influential individuals who can support and champion her initiatives. Taking the initiative to lead projects, propose new initiatives, or spearhead cross-department collaborations allows Maria to showcase her assertiveness and create meaningful opportunities that align with her vision and goals.

Negotiating Work-Life Balance:

Case Study: Jessica, a woman who values work-life balance, wants to assertively negotiate flexible working arrangements without compromising her career progression.

Strategy: Articulating Needs, Presenting Benefits, and Setting Boundaries

Jessica can assertively negotiate work-life balance by clearly articulating her needs, presenting the benefits of flexible working arrangements, and proposing solutions that address any potential concerns. By demonstrating how flexible arrangements can enhance productivity, job satisfaction, and overall well-being, Jessica can advocate for a healthier work-life integration. Setting clear boundaries and effectively communicating expectations with colleagues and supervisors will help Jessica maintain a healthy balance while continuing to excel in her career.

Assertiveness is a powerful tool for women to negotiate salary, promotions, and opportunities. By employing strategies such as research, preparation, effective communication, self-advocacy, documented achievements, building relationships, pitching ideas, networking, taking initiative, and setting boundaries, women can assert themselves confidently and achieve their professional goals. Embracing assertiveness in negotiation empowers women to secure fair compensation, pursue career advancements, and create meaningful opportunities that align with their aspirations. By harnessing the power of assertiveness, women can break barriers, challenge gender inequalities, and forge successful paths in their professional journeys.

Handling difficult conversations and managing conflicts

Difficult conversations and conflicts are inevitable in both personal and professional settings. For women, assertiveness is a valuable skill that can help navigate these challenging situations with confidence and effectiveness. We explore strategies and case studies that illustrate how assertiveness can be utilized to handle difficult conversations and manage conflicts, enabling women to maintain healthy relationships and resolve conflicts constructively.

Expressing Disagreements:
Case Study: Sarah, a woman who disagrees with a colleague's approach in a team project, wants

to express her concerns assertively without damaging the working relationship.

Strategy: Active Listening and Constructive Feedback

Sarah can begin by actively listening to her colleague's perspective, acknowledging their ideas, and demonstrating empathy. This sets the stage for open and respectful communication. When expressing her disagreement, Sarah can use "I" statements to share her perspective and provide constructive feedback. By focusing on the issue at hand rather than attacking the person, Sarah can assert herself while maintaining a collaborative and solution-oriented approach.

Setting Boundaries:

Case Study: Emily, a woman dealing with a colleague who consistently violates her personal boundaries, wants to assertively address the issue without causing unnecessary conflict.

Strategy: Firmly Asserting Boundaries and Active Conflict Resolution

Emily can assertively address the boundary violation by clearly and firmly communicating her limits and expectations. Using assertive language, she can express her discomfort and assert her need for respect. Additionally, active conflict resolution techniques, such as seeking a compromise or involving a neutral mediator, can help address the issue effectively while maintaining professionalism and preserving the working relationship.

Handling Feedback:

Case Study: Maria, a woman receiving critical feedback from her supervisor, wants to respond assertively without becoming defensive or demotivated.

Strategy: Active Listening, Self-Reflection, and Assertive Response

Maria can approach the feedback assertively by actively listening to her supervisor's perspective without becoming defensive. After reflecting on the feedback, she can respond assertively by acknowledging the areas for improvement, asking for clarification if needed, and sharing her own perspective. By maintaining a growth mindset and focusing on constructive solutions, Maria can turn the feedback into an opportunity for growth and professional development.

Managing Conflicts:

Case Study: Jessica, a woman involved in a conflict with a coworker, wants to assertively address the conflict and find a mutually acceptable resolution.

Strategy: Open Communication, Active Problem-Solving, and Collaboration

Jessica can manage the conflict assertively by initiating an open and honest conversation with her coworker. She can express her concerns, actively listen to the other person's perspective, and work towards a solution through active problem-solving and collaboration. By focusing on shared goals and mutual interests, Jessica can assert herself while promoting a cooperative and harmonious work environment.

Handling difficult conversations and managing conflicts assertively empowers women to navigate challenging situations with grace and effectiveness. By employing strategies such as active listening, constructive feedback, boundary-setting, active conflict resolution, assertive response to feedback, and collaborative problem-solving, women can assert themselves confidently while preserving relationships and promoting positive outcomes. Assertiveness in conflict management allows women to resolve conflicts constructively, foster understanding, and maintain healthy and productive relationships in both personal and professional spheres. By mastering the art of difficult conversations, women can create a positive impact and pave the way for effective communication and conflict resolution.

4.2 Assertiveness in Relationships:

Setting boundaries and expressing needs in personal relationships.

Setting boundaries and effectively expressing needs are essential aspects of healthy personal relationships. For women, assertiveness is a powerful tool that enables them to communicate their boundaries and express their needs with clarity and confidence.

Establishing Boundaries:

Case Study: Sarah, a woman in a close friendship, wants to establish boundaries regarding personal space and time without jeopardizing the relationship.
Strategy: Clear Communication and Consistent Reinforcement

Sarah can assertively communicate her boundaries by expressing her needs directly and clearly. For example, she can say, "I value our friendship, but I also need some alone time to recharge. Can we schedule some dedicated 'me' time?" By openly discussing her boundaries and the reasons behind them, Sarah fosters understanding and respect within the friendship. Consistently reinforcing these boundaries ensures that her needs are met while maintaining a strong and balanced relationship.

Expressing Emotional Needs:
Case Study: Emily, a woman in a romantic relationship, wants to assertively express her emotional needs to her partner without feeling vulnerable or dependent.
Strategy: "I" Statements and Active Listening

Emily can express her emotional needs assertively by using "I" statements, such as "I feel loved and appreciated when we spend quality time together." By focusing on her own feelings and experiences, Emily communicates her needs without blaming or criticizing her partner. Active listening also plays a crucial role in fostering effective communication. By listening to her partner's perspective and encouraging open dialogue, Emily creates a safe space for both individuals to express their needs and strengthen their emotional connection.

Negotiating Household Responsibilities:
Case Study: Maria, a woman in a committed partnership, wants to assertively negotiate and distribute household responsibilities in a fair and balanced manner.

Strategy: Open Communication and Collaborative Problem-Solving

Maria can assertively address household responsibilities by initiating an open and honest conversation with her partner. By expressing her needs and concerns, she can work together with her partner to find a fair distribution of tasks. Using collaborative problem-solving techniques, such as creating a shared task list or alternating responsibilities, Maria ensures that both partners contribute equally and that their needs and preferences are taken into consideration.

Asserting Personal Values:

Case Study: Jessica, a woman with strong personal values, wants to assertively express her boundaries and expectations regarding certain behaviors or topics in her friendships.
Strategy: Honest Communication and Respectful Assertiveness

Jessica can assertively express her personal values by engaging in honest and open communication with her friends. By expressing her boundaries and expectations regarding certain behaviors or topics, Jessica establishes a foundation of respect and understanding. For example, she can say, "I value our friendship, but it's important to me that we avoid discussing sensitive political issues." By communicating assertively, Jessica ensures that her friendships are built on mutual respect and shared values.

Assertiveness empowers women to set boundaries and express their needs effectively in personal relationships. By employing strategies such as clear communication, "I" statements, active listening, open dialogue, collaborative problem-solving, and respectful assertiveness, women can establish healthy boundaries, cultivate meaningful connections, and foster fulfilling personal relationships. Assertive communication allows women to assert their needs, express their values, and maintain respectful relationships built on trust and understanding. By embracing assertiveness, women can create spaces where their boundaries are respected, their needs are met, and their personal relationships thrive.

Nurturing Assertiveness in Intimate Partnerships

Managing assertiveness within intimate partnerships is crucial for fostering healthy communication, maintaining mutual respect, and promoting personal growth. For women, assertiveness serves as a valuable tool to express needs, set boundaries, and navigate relationship dynamics with confidence and compassion.

Open and Honest Communication:
Case Study: Sarah and John, a couple facing challenges in their communication patterns, want to establish assertive communication to deepen their emotional connection.
Strategy: Active Listening and Non-Defensive Expression

Sarah and John can foster assertiveness in their partnership by actively listening to each other's perspectives without judgment or defensiveness. By encouraging open dialogue and practicing active listening techniques, such as paraphrasing and summarizing each other's thoughts, they can ensure that both partners feel heard and understood. Non-defensive expression allows them to assert their needs and emotions in a respectful manner, fostering a safe space for open communication and mutual growth.

Setting Boundaries:
Case Study: Emily and Alex, a couple struggling with personal space and individual interests, want to assertively establish boundaries to nurture their individual identities within the relationship.
Strategy: Clear Communication and Negotiation

Emily and Alex can assertively set boundaries by openly discussing their individual needs and expectations. Through clear communication, they can negotiate and establish guidelines that honor their personal space and individual interests. By proactively addressing potential challenges and finding mutually satisfying solutions, they can create a balance that allows both partners to thrive independently while maintaining a strong and supportive partnership.

Expressing Intimacy and Emotional Needs:

Case Study: Maria and Lisa, a same-sex couple, want to assertively express their intimacy and emotional needs to deepen their connection and ensure mutual fulfillment.
Strategy: Vulnerability and Mutual Support

Maria and Lisa can assertively express their intimacy and emotional needs by cultivating vulnerability and mutual support within their relationship. By openly sharing their desires, preferences, and boundaries, they create a space for emotional growth and understanding. Active support and validation of each other's emotions foster trust, allowing both partners to assert their needs confidently while strengthening the emotional bond they share.

Managing Conflict:

Case Study: Jessica and Ryan, a couple experiencing frequent conflicts, want to

assertively manage their differences and resolve conflicts constructively.
Strategy: Active Conflict Resolution and Empathy

Jessica and Ryan can manage conflicts assertively by engaging in active conflict resolution strategies. This includes identifying the underlying issues, listening actively to each other's perspectives, and seeking collaborative solutions. By practicing empathy and understanding, they can navigate differences with compassion, finding common ground and maintaining a healthy and harmonious partnership.

Managing assertiveness within intimate partnerships empowers women to establish effective communication, set boundaries, express needs, and resolve conflicts constructively. By implementing strategies such as open and honest communication, boundary-setting, expressing intimacy and emotional needs, and managing conflict assertively, women can nurture healthy and fulfilling intimate relationships. Embracing assertiveness in intimate partnerships cultivates a foundation of mutual respect, empathy, and growth, allowing women to thrive personally and within the context of a loving and supportive partnership. By empowering themselves through assertive communication, women can create enduring and fulfilling connections with their partners.

Handling conflicts and disagreements constructively

Conflicts and disagreements are inevitable in both personal and professional relationships. For women, assertiveness is a powerful tool that enables them to handle conflicts constructively, fostering understanding, collaboration, and growth. We explore strategies and case studies that demonstrate how assertiveness can be utilized to navigate conflicts and disagreements, empowering women to build healthier relationships and achieve positive outcomes.

Active Listening and Empathy:

Case Study: Sarah, a woman facing a conflict with a coworker, wants to address the issue assertively and find a resolution.
Strategy: Active Listening, Understanding Perspectives, and Empathetic Responses

Sarah can begin by actively listening to her coworker's concerns and perspectives, demonstrating genuine interest and empathy. By seeking to understand the underlying reasons behind the conflict, Sarah can engage in a constructive dialogue that focuses on finding common ground. Through empathetic responses, such as acknowledging the coworker's feelings and validating their experiences, Sarah establishes a foundation of trust and respect, leading to a more productive resolution.

Clear Communication and "I" Statements:
Case Study: Emily, a woman experiencing a disagreement with her partner, wants to assertively express her perspective and find a compromise.

Strategy: Clear Expression of Feelings and "I" Statements

Emily can assertively handle the disagreement by clearly expressing her feelings and needs using "I" statements. For example, she can say, "I feel frustrated when this happens because it makes me think my opinions are not valued." By using "I" statements, Emily takes ownership of her emotions and avoids sounding accusatory. This approach fosters open communication and encourages her partner to understand her perspective, leading to a constructive conversation and a potential compromise.

Problem-Solving and Collaboration:
Case Study: Maria, a woman dealing with a conflict in a team project, wants to assertively resolve the issue and maintain a positive working environment.
Strategy: Collaborative Problem-Solving and Solution-Oriented Approach

Maria can assertively handle the conflict by focusing on problem-solving and collaboration.

She can initiate a team discussion to identify the root cause of the conflict and brainstorm potential solutions. By actively involving team members in the decision-making process and valuing their input, Maria fosters a sense of ownership and collective responsibility. This approach encourages a positive and solution-oriented atmosphere, enabling the team to move forward and achieve their goals.

Emotional Regulation and Conflict De-escalation:

Case Study: Jessica, a woman involved in a heated disagreement with a friend, wants to assertively manage her emotions and de-escalate the conflict.

Strategy: Emotional Regulation, Time-Outs, and Calm Discussions

Jessica can assertively handle the conflict by practicing emotional regulation techniques. If emotions are running high, she can suggest taking a time-out to cool down before resuming the discussion. During the calm discussion, Jessica can express her thoughts and feelings assertively while actively listening to her friend's perspective. By maintaining a calm and composed demeanor, Jessica promotes a respectful and constructive conversation, facilitating the resolution of the conflict.

Handling conflicts and disagreements constructively through assertiveness empowers women to build stronger relationships and achieve positive outcomes. By employing strategies such as active listening, empathy, clear communication using "I" statements, problem-solving, collaboration, emotional regulation, and conflict de-escalation, women can navigate conflicts assertively and promote understanding, growth, and resolution. Embracing assertiveness in conflict resolution allows women to express their perspectives, address issues effectively, and foster healthier and more fulfilling relationships. Through the power of assertiveness, women can transform conflicts into opportunities for personal and interpersonal growth

Chapter 5

Overcoming Barriers and Obstacles

Common Obstacles to Assertiveness for Women

Assertiveness is a valuable skill that enables individuals to express their thoughts, needs, and boundaries effectively. However, women often face specific obstacles that can hinder their ability to assert themselves confidently. Understanding these obstacles is crucial for developing strategies to overcome them.

Societal Gender Stereotypes:
Women often encounter societal expectations and stereotypes that may discourage assertiveness. Cultural norms that promote women as passive, nurturing, or accommodating can create barriers to assertive behavior. Society's expectations may lead to self-doubt, fear of being perceived as

aggressive, or the belief that women should prioritize others' needs over their own.

Fear of Negative Evaluation:
Women, more so than men, tend to fear negative evaluation and social repercussions when expressing assertiveness. This fear of being judged or labeled as "bossy" or "aggressive" can lead women to avoid asserting their opinions, needs, or boundaries. The desire to maintain harmony and be liked can override their willingness to assert themselves.

Lack of Role Models:
The scarcity of assertive female role models in leadership positions can hinder women's belief in their own assertiveness. Limited visibility of successful assertive women can make it difficult for women to envision themselves as capable of being assertive in various situations. The absence of relatable role models may contribute to self-doubt and feelings of isolation.

Cultural and Diversity Factors:
Different cultural backgrounds and societal norms can influence the perception and

acceptance of assertiveness. Cultural expectations may vary, and some women may face additional challenges due to their ethnicity, race, or religious beliefs. These factors can impact the way assertiveness is perceived and accepted within specific communities or cultural contexts.

Lack of Self-Confidence and Self-Esteem:

Low self-confidence and self-esteem can undermine a woman's assertiveness. When individuals do not believe in their own worth or abilities, they may hesitate to assert themselves, fearing rejection or being seen as undeserving. Developing self-confidence and recognizing one's value are essential for cultivating assertive behavior.

Past Negative Experiences:

Negative experiences, such as being dismissed, ignored, or undermined, can diminish a woman's assertiveness. Previous instances of being shut down or facing backlash for speaking up can create a fear of recurrence, discouraging future assertive behavior. Overcoming these past experiences is crucial for reclaiming one's assertiveness.

Recognizing the common obstacles to assertiveness for women is the first step in overcoming them. By challenging societal stereotypes, building self-confidence, seeking positive role models, and reframing negative experiences, women can embrace their assertive voices. Empowering women to express themselves confidently and assertively fosters personal growth, enhances professional success, and promotes gender equality. With determination, self-awareness, and support, women can navigate these obstacles and cultivate assertiveness in all areas of their lives.

Overcoming Fear, Guilt, and Social Conditioning

In a society that has long perpetuated gender stereotypes and societal expectations, it can be challenging for women to assert themselves confidently and authentically. Fear, guilt, and social conditioning often act as barriers, hindering women from expressing their thoughts, needs, and desires assertively.

However, by adopting effective strategies and empowering oneself, women can break free from these constraints and embrace their assertiveness.

Recognize and Challenge Internalized Fear:

Fear often stems from internalized beliefs and societal conditioning, leading women to doubt their abilities and hesitate to express themselves assertively. To overcome this, it is crucial to recognize the fear and question its validity. Reflect on past experiences where fear may have held you back and challenge the negative assumptions associated with it. Remember, fear is often a result of conditioning rather than an accurate reflection of reality.

Cultivate Self-Confidence:

Building self-confidence is key to overcoming fear and embracing assertiveness. Focus on your strengths and accomplishments, and remind yourself of the value you bring to any situation. Engage in self-care practices that promote self-acceptance, such as positive affirmations, visualization exercises, and maintaining a healthy lifestyle. Surround yourself with supportive individuals who uplift and encourage you to believe in yourself.

Practice Self-Compassion and Release Guilt:

Guilt is a common emotion that can weigh heavily on women when asserting themselves. It is essential to practice self-compassion and understand that prioritizing your needs and setting boundaries is not selfish but necessary for personal growth. Recognize that guilt often stems from societal expectations and ingrained gender roles. Reframe guilt as an opportunity to establish healthier boundaries and advocate for your own well-being.

Challenge Social Conditioning:

Social conditioning plays a significant role in shaping gender roles and expectations. Recognize the impact of societal norms on your behavior and thought patterns. Examine the messages you have internalized and challenge their validity. Surround yourself with empowering role models who defy traditional gender stereotypes and inspire you to embrace your own authentic voice. Engage in personal development activities such as reading, attending workshops, or joining support groups to further challenge social conditioning and expand your perspectives.

Develop Effective Communication Skills:
Effective communication is an essential component of assertiveness. Invest time in developing your communication skills, including active listening, clear articulation, and non-verbal cues. Practice expressing your thoughts and needs assertively, using "I" statements to convey your perspective while remaining respectful of others. Seek opportunities to engage in public speaking, negotiation, or conflict resolution, as these experiences can bolster your confidence in expressing yourself assertively.

Set Clear Boundaries:
Establishing and maintaining healthy boundaries is crucial for assertiveness. Clearly define your limits and communicate them confidently. Be prepared to say "no" when necessary, without feeling the need to justify or

apologize excessively. Remember, your boundaries are valid, and respecting them is crucial for your overall well-being.

Overcoming fear, guilt, and social conditioning is an empowering journey that allows women to embrace their assertiveness and lead fulfilling lives. By recognizing and challenging internalized beliefs, cultivating self-confidence, practicing self-compassion, challenging social conditioning, developing effective communication skills, and setting clear boundaries, women can break free from the constraints that hold them back. Remember, your assertiveness is your superpower, and by embracing it, you can inspire others and create positive change in your personal and professional spheres. Empower yourself and pave the way for a more inclusive and equal world

Building Resilience: Overcoming Setbacks

Assertiveness is a powerful tool for women to express their needs, opinions, and boundaries. However, setbacks are an inevitable part of any journey, and developing resilience is crucial in overcoming these challenges and continuing to cultivate assertiveness. Through real-life case studies and practical strategies, we will explore how women can bounce back from setbacks and emerge stronger than ever.

Case Study 1: Overcoming Self-Doubt
Sarah, a talented professional, often found herself doubting her abilities and hesitant to assert her opinions in team meetings. This self-doubt hindered her professional growth and undermined her confidence. However, Sarah decided to address her setback head-on and develop resilience.

Strategy 1: Embrace Growth Mindset
Sarah recognized that her self-doubt stemmed from a fixed mindset, where she believed her abilities were set in stone. By embracing a growth mindset, she understood that her skills and assertiveness could be developed over time. Sarah focused on personal growth, seeking out opportunities for skill enhancement and learning from her setbacks.

Strategy 2: Seek Support and Feedback
Sarah sought guidance from a mentor who provided valuable insights and feedback on her assertiveness. This external perspective helped her identify her strengths and areas for improvement. By surrounding herself with supportive individuals, Sarah gained a sense of reassurance and encouragement to overcome her setbacks.

Case Study 2: Bouncing Back from Rejection

Linda, a passionate entrepreneur, faced multiple rejections when seeking funding for her business venture. These setbacks not only challenged her assertiveness but also tested her resilience and determination.

Strategy 1: Reframe Failure as Learning Opportunities
Instead of viewing rejections as personal failures, Linda reframed them as valuable learning opportunities. She analyzed each setback, identifying areas for improvement and fine-tuning her business pitch. By embracing a growth mindset, Linda continued to refine her

assertiveness skills and adapt to the feedback received.

Strategy 2: Persistence and Resilience
Linda maintained her belief in her business idea and persisted despite setbacks. She utilized her network to explore alternative funding sources and sought advice from successful entrepreneurs who faced similar challenges. Linda's resilience enabled her to overcome the setbacks and eventually secure funding for her venture.

Case Study 3: Navigating Conflict
Rachel, a dedicated team leader, faced a conflict situation where her assertiveness was met with resistance and pushback from team members. This setback caused her to question her approach and authority.

Strategy 1: Reflect and Adjust Communication Style
Rachel took time to reflect on her communication style and how it may have contributed to the conflict. She assessed her assertiveness levels and considered adapting

her approach to align better with the team's dynamics. By remaining open to feedback and making necessary adjustments, Rachel improved her assertiveness and conflict resolution skills.

Strategy 2: Seek Mediation and Conflict Resolution Techniques
To address the conflict, Rachel sought the assistance of a trained mediator who facilitated open dialogue and encouraged active listening among team members. By engaging in constructive conversations and utilizing conflict resolution techniques, Rachel was able to navigate the setback and foster a more assertive and collaborative work environment.

Building resilience in the face of setbacks is crucial for women aiming to cultivate assertiveness. By embracing a growth mindset, seeking support and feedback, reframing failure as learning opportunities, persisting in the face of challenges, reflecting and adjusting communication styles, and utilizing conflict resolution techniques, women can overcome setbacks and emerge stronger in their assertiveness journey. These case studies highlight the power of resilience and provide practical strategies for women to navigate obstacles with grace, confidence.

5.1 Assertiveness and Self-Care:

The Power of Self-Care

In the pursuit of assertiveness, women often find themselves neglecting their own well-being. However, recognizing the importance of self-care is vital for maintaining and nurturing assertiveness. Self-care encompasses various practices that prioritize physical, mental, and emotional health, allowing women to cultivate a strong foundation from which their assertiveness can flourish.

Understanding the Connection:
Self-care and assertiveness share an intimate relationship. When women prioritize self-care, they replenish their physical and emotional energy, enhance self-esteem, and cultivate a sense of inner strength. This foundation is

crucial for confidently asserting one's needs, boundaries, and opinions. Recognizing the connection between self-care and assertiveness allows women to approach both aspects of their lives holistically.

Prioritizing Physical Health:

Physical well-being forms the cornerstone of self-care. Engaging in regular exercise, maintaining a balanced diet, and getting sufficient sleep are essential for overall vitality and assertiveness. Exercise releases endorphins, boosting mood and self-confidence. Proper nutrition provides the energy needed to tackle challenges assertively. Sufficient rest fosters mental clarity and emotional resilience. Prioritizing physical health ensures women are equipped to navigate assertive situations with vigor and determination.

Nurturing Emotional Well-being:

Emotional self-care is vital for maintaining assertiveness. Women should allocate time for activities that bring joy and relaxation, such as hobbies, creative pursuits, or spending time with loved ones. Practicing mindfulness and emotional awareness helps in identifying and addressing emotional needs. Journaling, therapy, or support groups can provide safe spaces for emotional expression. By nurturing emotional well-being, women develop a solid emotional foundation from which they can assert themselves confidently and authentically.

Setting Boundaries and Saying No:
Self-care involves setting boundaries and recognizing the importance of saying no when necessary. Women often feel compelled to accommodate others' needs, leading to burnout and compromised assertiveness. By setting clear boundaries, they protect their time, energy, and personal space. Saying no respectfully but firmly allows for the preservation of personal well-being and enables women to prioritize their assertive communication and actions.

Cultivating Self-Compassion:
Self-compassion is a vital aspect of self-care. It involves treating oneself with kindness, understanding, and acceptance. Women should

embrace self-compassion when facing setbacks or moments of self-doubt. Instead of criticizing themselves, they can offer self-care practices like positive affirmations, self-reflection, and self-forgiveness. By cultivating self-compassion, women build resilience, boost self-esteem, and maintain the motivation to assert themselves confidently.

Engaging in Relaxation Techniques:
Amidst the demands of life, women must incorporate relaxation techniques into their self-care routine. Engaging in activities such as meditation, deep breathing exercises, yoga, or taking soothing baths promotes relaxation, reduces stress, and rejuvenates the mind and body. Relaxation techniques foster emotional balance, allowing women to approach assertive situations with clarity and composure.

Recognizing the importance of self-care is vital for women aiming to cultivate assertiveness. Prioritizing physical health, nurturing emotional well-being, setting boundaries and saying no, cultivating self-compassion, and engaging in relaxation techniques all contribute to a strong foundation for assertive expression. By embracing self-care practices, women empower themselves, foster resilience, and establish the necessary balance to navigate life's challenges assertively. Remember, self-care is not selfish but an essential investment in your own well-being, enabling you to assert yourself

Finding Balance: Managing Stress and Burnout

Assertiveness is a powerful tool for women to express themselves confidently and authentically. However, the pursuit of assertiveness can sometimes lead to stress and burnout, as the demands of navigating challenging situations and societal expectations take a toll. Managing stress and preventing burnout is crucial for maintaining long-term assertiveness and overall well-being. Through a real-life case study and practical strategies, we will explore how women can navigate the challenges of assertiveness while prioritizing self-care.

Case Study: Sarah's Journey to Balance
Sarah, a driven professional, experienced high levels of stress and burnout due to the constant pressure to assert herself in a competitive work environment. She recognized the need to manage her stress and prevent burnout in order to maintain her assertiveness effectively.

Strategy 1: Prioritize Self-Care and Work-Life Balance
Sarah realized the importance of self-care and creating a healthy work-life balance. She started by setting clear boundaries between work and personal life, allowing herself dedicated time for rest, relaxation, and activities she enjoyed. Sarah made self-care a non-negotiable priority, which included engaging in hobbies, practicing mindfulness, and spending quality time with loved ones. By prioritizing self-care, Sarah replenished her energy and built resilience to manage stress effectively.

Strategy 2: Practice Stress Management Techniques
Sarah incorporated stress management techniques into her daily routine. She explored

different methods, such as deep breathing exercises, meditation, and regular physical activity, to reduce stress levels. By regularly engaging in these techniques, Sarah improved her ability to cope with stress and maintain a calm and focused mindset. These practices not only helped her manage stress in assertive situations but also promoted her overall well-being.

Strategy 3: Delegate and Seek Support

Recognizing the importance of support, Sarah learned to delegate tasks and seek assistance when needed. She realized that she did not have to handle everything alone. Sarah effectively communicated her needs and limitations to her colleagues and superiors, allowing for a more balanced distribution of workload. By seeking support, Sarah lightened her burden and created space for assertiveness without overwhelming herself.

Strategy 4: Time Management and Prioritization

Sarah developed strong time management skills and learned to prioritize tasks effectively. She created to-do lists, identified urgent and important tasks, and delegated or eliminated nonessential responsibilities. By organizing her time efficiently, Sarah reduced stress, improved productivity, and created a conducive environment for assertiveness.

Strategy 5: Regular Self-Reflection and Evaluation

Sarah regularly reflected on her assertiveness journey, assessing her progress and identifying areas for improvement. Through self-reflection, she gained insight into her triggers, stressors, and warning signs of burnout. This self-awareness allowed her to proactively address potential stressors and make necessary adjustments to her approach. Sarah celebrated her achievements and acknowledged her growth, further motivating her to continue her journey towards assertiveness.

Managing stress and preventing burnout is vital for women striving to maintain assertiveness. By prioritizing self-care and work-life balance, practicing stress management techniques, delegating and seeking support, mastering time management and prioritization, and engaging in regular self-reflection and evaluation, women can effectively navigate the challenges of assertiveness while preserving their well-being. Sarah's case study demonstrates the power of these strategies in finding balance and fostering resilience. Remember, assertiveness is not about sacrificing your well-being, but rather about expressing yourself confidently while prioritizing self-care and maintaining a healthy equilibrium.

Unapologetic Self-Care: Prioritizing Personal Well-being

In the pursuit of assertiveness, women often face the challenge of balancing personal well-being with societal expectations and responsibilities. However, it is essential for women to prioritize their personal well-being without guilt, as it forms the foundation for confident and authentic assertiveness.

Case Study 1: Emma's Journey to Self-Care

Emma, a dedicated working professional and a mother, often found herself neglecting her personal well-being in her pursuit of assertiveness. However, she realized the importance of prioritizing self-care to maintain her assertive nature effectively.

Strategy 1: Redefine Self-Care

Emma recognized that self-care is not selfish but necessary for her overall well-being and assertiveness. She reframed self-care as an act of self-preservation and empowerment, understanding that prioritizing herself positively impacts all aspects of her life, including her ability to assert herself confidently.

Strategy 2: Establish Boundaries

Emma learned to set boundaries and communicate her needs effectively. She clearly defined her limits and communicated them assertively to others, ensuring that she had dedicated time and space for self-care activities. By establishing boundaries, Emma preserved her personal well-being and created a foundation for maintaining her assertiveness.

Case Study 2: Maya's Pursuit of Balance

Maya, an ambitious professional, often felt guilty when prioritizing her personal well-being over work-related demands. However, she realized that guilt was hindering her assertiveness and decided to make a change.

Strategy 1: Challenge Societal Expectations

Maya examined societal expectations and realized that they often perpetuated the idea that women should put their own needs last. She challenged these expectations and embraced the belief that prioritizing personal well-being is not only acceptable but necessary for her overall success and assertiveness. By defying societal norms, Maya freed herself from guilt and embraced unapologetic self-care.

Strategy 2: Foster a Supportive Network

Maya surrounded herself with a supportive network of individuals who encouraged and validated her pursuit of personal well-being.

She connected with like-minded individuals who shared similar challenges and aspirations, creating a community that uplifted and celebrated self-care. This support network reinforced her belief in the importance of prioritizing personal well-being without guilt.

Prioritizing personal well-being without guilt is essential for women aiming to cultivate assertiveness. By redefining self-care, establishing boundaries, challenging societal expectations, fostering a supportive network, and embracing unapologetic self-care, women can prioritize themselves and nurture their well-being. The case studies of Emma and Maya illustrate the transformative power of these strategies in reclaiming personal well-being and maintaining assertiveness. Remember, prioritizing yourself is not a selfish act, but rather an empowering choice that allows you to show up confidently and authentically in all aspects of your life. Embrace self-care unapologetically and watch as your assertiveness thrives.

5.2 Seeking Support and Building a Network:

Developing a Support System of Like-Minded Individuals

In a world where women continue to strive for equality and recognition, cultivating assertiveness is a crucial skill. Being assertive allows women to confidently express their thoughts, needs, and boundaries, enabling them to navigate both personal and professional relationships effectively. However, the journey towards assertiveness can be challenging and often requires a support system. Building a network of like-minded individuals who understand and encourage assertiveness can provide invaluable guidance and empowerment.

Understanding the Power of a Support System:

A. Validation and Empathy: Surrounding oneself with like-minded individuals creates a safe space to express concerns, fears, and triumphs. Sharing experiences with others who face similar challenges can validate one's feelings and provide a sense of empathy that fosters personal growth and self-acceptance.

B. Encouragement and Motivation: A support system offers encouragement and motivation, which are vital in moments of self-doubt. Like-minded individuals can share success stories, offer advice, and provide motivation during times when assertiveness feels difficult.

C. Learning from Shared Knowledge: Connecting with individuals who share a common goal of assertiveness allows for the exchange of knowledge and experiences. Learning from others' journeys and strategies can significantly enhance personal growth and development.

Building Your Support System:
A. Identify Your Values and Goals: Start by clarifying your personal values and assertiveness goals. Reflect on what you hope to achieve through assertiveness and the qualities you seek in a support network.

B. Seek Out Like-Minded Communities:
Explore local organizations, professional networks, or online communities that focus on empowering women and developing assertiveness. These communities can provide a platform to connect with individuals who share similar values and aspirations.

C. Attend Workshops and Events:
Participating in workshops, seminars, or conferences centered around assertiveness and women's empowerment can be an excellent opportunity to meet like-minded individuals and expand your network.

D. Engage in Online Platforms: Social media groups, forums, and online discussion platforms dedicated to assertiveness and women's empowerment can connect you with a diverse range of individuals who are passionate about the same topics.

E. Network with Purpose: Actively engage with individuals within your support system by attending events, initiating conversations, and seeking out mentorship opportunities. Be open to forming meaningful connections and nurturing relationships.

Nurturing and Sustaining Your Support System:

A. Regular Communication: Regularly connect with individuals within your support system through group meetings, one-on-one conversations, or virtual meetups. Establishing consistent communication fosters trust, understanding, and ongoing support.

B. Share Experiences and Knowledge: Be open to sharing your own experiences, challenges, and triumphs. By doing so, you create a reciprocal environment where others feel comfortable sharing their own stories and insights.

C. Collaborative Learning: Organize workshops, book clubs, or skill-sharing sessions within your support system. Encourage members to share their expertise and create a collective learning environment that benefits everyone.

D. Celebrate Achievements: Acknowledge and celebrate individual and collective achievements within your support system. Recognize the milestones reached and provide encouragement to keep progressing towards assertiveness.

Developing a support system of like-minded individuals in assertiveness as a woman is a powerful tool for personal growth and empowerment. By surrounding yourself with individuals who understand and encourage assertiveness, you can navigate challenges more effectively, learn from shared experiences, and find the motivation to persevere. Building and nurturing such a support system requires proactive engagement, consistent communication, and a willingness to share.

Encouraging and Empowering Women to Embrace Assertiveness

In a world where gender equality remains an ongoing battle, it is crucial for women to break free from societal constraints and embrace assertiveness. Assertiveness empowers women to express their opinions, stand up for themselves, and pursue their goals with confidence. By encouraging and supporting one another, we can create an environment that fosters women's assertiveness and propels us towards greater success and fulfillment.

Understanding the Power of Assertiveness:

Assertiveness is often misconstrued as aggression or bossiness. However, it is a fundamental communication skill that allows women to express their needs, desires, and boundaries effectively. Assertive women possess the courage to voice their opinions, negotiate for fair treatment, and take on leadership roles. By embracing assertiveness, women can overcome gender biases, break through glass ceilings, and create positive change in their personal and professional lives.

Celebrating the Successes of Assertive Women:

To encourage and empower other women to be assertive, we must celebrate the successes of assertive women. Highlighting the achievements of women who have confidently pursued their goals and made significant contributions not only serves as inspiration but also dismantles the stereotype that assertiveness is incompatible with femininity. By sharing these stories, we create a narrative that empowers women to be assertive without fear of judgment or backlash.

Building a Supportive Network:

Support networks play a vital role in fostering assertiveness among women. By creating spaces where women can share their experiences, challenges, and triumphs, we can cultivate a supportive environment that encourages assertiveness. Establishing mentorship programs, professional organizations, or affinity groups that prioritize the development and advancement of women can provide valuable guidance and empowerment. In these spaces, women can learn from one another, exchange strategies, and gain the confidence to assert themselves.

Providing Skills Training and Education:

To be assertive, women need the necessary skills and knowledge to navigate various professional situations. Employers and organizations can contribute by offering workshops and training programs that focus on communication, negotiation, and conflict resolution skills. Equipping women with these tools empowers them to assert their opinions, set boundaries, and advocate for themselves effectively. Investing in women's professional development helps cultivate a culture of assertiveness and paves the way for gender equality in the workplace.

Challenging Stereotypes and Bias:

As women, we must challenge stereotypes and biases that hinder assertiveness. By recognizing and addressing these societal expectations, we can redefine the concept of femininity and assertiveness. Encouraging women to step outside traditional gender roles and embrace their own unique leadership styles is essential. Together, we can break down barriers and create a more inclusive environment that values and celebrates assertive women.

Encouraging and empowering women to be assertive is an essential step towards achieving gender equality. By embracing assertiveness, women can confidently pursue their goals, contribute meaningfully, and make their voices heard. By celebrating successes, building supportive networks, providing skills training, and challenging stereotypes, we can create a professional environment where women feel empowered to be assertive without fear or hesitation. Let us uplift and support one another, fostering a culture that empowers women to step into their full potential and thrive.

Collaborating with Mentors and Role Models

Assertiveness is a vital skill that empowers women to navigate professional challenges, overcome obstacles, and achieve their goals. While developing assertiveness requires personal effort and determination, collaborating with mentors and role models can significantly enhance this journey. Mentors and role models offer guidance, support, and valuable insights based on their own experiences. We will explore the significance of collaborating with mentors and role models in cultivating assertiveness as a woman, and provide practical tips for establishing and nurturing these valuable relationships.

Recognizing the Power of Mentors and Role Models:

Mentors and role models serve as invaluable sources of inspiration and guidance for women seeking to develop assertiveness. Mentors are experienced individuals who provide personalized advice, share their expertise, and help navigate career challenges. Role models, on the other hand, can be admired from afar, offering inspiration and motivation through their achievements and values. Both mentors and role models can play a transformative role in fostering assertiveness by imparting wisdom, sharing experiences, and serving as a source of encouragement.

Seeking Out Mentors and Role Models:

To collaborate with mentors and role models effectively, it is essential to proactively seek out these relationships. Look for individuals who have achieved success in your desired field or who possess the assertiveness you admire. Seek out opportunities such as networking events, conferences, or professional organizations where you can connect with potential mentors and role models. Additionally, online platforms and communities dedicated to professional development can provide avenues for building these relationships.

Building Authentic Relationships:
When approaching potential mentors and role models, focus on building authentic relationships grounded in mutual respect and trust. Take the time to understand their background, achievements, and values. Show genuine interest in their work and seek their advice on specific areas you wish to develop assertiveness in. Actively listen to their insights, perspectives, and stories, and demonstrate gratitude for their time and wisdom.

Establishing Clear Communication Channels:
Clear communication is vital for successful collaboration with mentors and role models. Set expectations early on regarding the frequency and mode of communication. Whether it's through regular meetings, emails, or phone calls, establish a communication routine that works for both parties. Be proactive in seeking feedback and guidance, and provide updates on

your progress and challenges. Effective communication will ensure a strong and meaningful mentoring relationship.

Emulating and Learning from Mentors and Role Models:

Observing and learning from mentors and role models is crucial for developing assertiveness. Pay attention to their communication style, negotiation techniques, and problem-solving approaches. Emulate the qualities you admire while adapting them to your own personality and circumstances. Reflect on their experiences and how they handle assertiveness challenges. Extract lessons and apply them to your own professional journey.

Leveraging Opportunities for Growth:

Mentors and role models can open doors to new opportunities for personal and professional growth. They may provide introductions to influential networks, recommend relevant resources, or even involve you in projects that enhance your assertiveness skills. Embrace these opportunities and actively seek ways to expand your skills and experiences under their guidance.

Collaborating with mentors and role models is a powerful strategy for women seeking to develop assertiveness in their professional lives. These relationships offer guidance, inspiration, and practical advice based on real-world experiences. By actively seeking out mentors and role models, building authentic relationships, establishing clear communication channels, and learning from their expertise, women can accelerate their assertiveness journey and achieve greater success and fulfillment. Embrace the power of collaboration, and let mentors and role models become your allies in unlocking your full potential as an assertive woman in the professional world.

The end